MW00623576

BOUNTY

Lopez Island Farmers, Food, and Community

Photographs by Robert S. Harrison, Steve Horn, and Summer Moon Scriver
Profiles by Iris Graville · Recipes by Kim Bast

....

Foreword by Vicki Robin, author of
Blessing the Hands That Feed Us: Lessons from a 10-Mile Diet

Table of Contents

Foreword

EATING IS BELIEVING. Nothing quells the voices of doom—inside our heads or from the chatter around us—like a little direct experience.

I'd lived for years with these dark voices. The bomb. The population bomb. If everyone lived as Americans we'd need two . . . or is it three . . . or four . . . planets to survive, and we have but one. And I didn't sit on my fears like a brood hen. No, I turned my fears into fire and tried to forge a different future by writing, speaking and influencing leaders.

In 2010, though, it all came home to roost. Living on an island (Whidbey) served by a ferry to the south and a narrow bridge to the north, I wondered how well we would eat if all else failed and we were left to our own devices. A farmer friend calculated the population of the island, times 2,000 calories a day, divided by the food calories we now grow on the farm land we have, and delivered doom on a platter: we'd survive for about two weeks in August.

After dithering like Chicken Little for a few crazy months, another farmer and I came up with a test plot (as in scheme): she'd feed me all the veggies I could eat, and I'd blog for food, documenting how well this one farmer could feed this one human. Being an omnivore, we agreed I could supplement with local meat. Given that she lived less than ten miles from me, we dubbed it the "ten-mile-diet." In September, we ran the experiment.

It was transformative. Let me count the ways.

I wrote and wrote and wrote, my posts first with an audience of three and eventually an audience of many thousands once the posts were composted and reborn as a book, *Blessing the Hands That Feed Us: Lessons from a 10-Mile Diet* (Viking Penguin 2014).

I learned to cook from ingredients rather than recipes—and to make basics like butter and salt from my ten-mile circle.

I bonded with my community—the farmers for sure, but also the forests and fields—feeling perhaps for the first time in my life that I actually belonged somewhere because I truly depended on this place for my life.

My destiny now tied to Whidbey, I worked to help rebuild our local, and eventually regional, food system. Local food, I discovered, is not a local food system. Ours was exquisite in the detail of effulgent lettuces or heirloom tomatoes but fragmented, insufficient, and hindered by market forces.

Speaking of dithering chickens, I saw how these global industrial market forces make local chicken expensive and grocery chicken cheap, which in terms of health, justice, resilience, and happy chickens is exactly the opposite of what it should be.

I knew experientially—including reading incessantly while I ate my local meals—that we don't need that global industrial corporate system to feed the world. Many studies say that agro-ecology (diverse, organic, small-scale farming) can do a better job if the global financial and resource extraction system would quit with the earth-ravaging already and support farmers everywhere staying home in their ten-mile circles.

I came to call all of this "relational eating." Local food is a product. Relational eating is the transformative process we go through when we commit to a place on earth as our source of nourishment.

Finally, the ten-mile diet restored my hope. Eating is believing. I saw for myself that we can do this! Focused on dire data, I had lost sight of a very real fact. We actually don't know how anything turns out. Life has a will to live beyond all imagining. Seed and soil and sun and water will, without human instructions, keep making life in whatever patches prove hospitable. Humans in community have been making the best of floods, ice ages, plagues, and more for at least ten million years, with prophets of doom in every era convincing people that the end is at hand.

The end of a hoe is where hope begins. Imagine my delight when I discovered that the plot I'd hatched in 2010 took root on another island and helped grow the BOUNTY Project, which now, in turn, feeds my hope and admiration.

And so I deliver to you, on a beautifully carved red cedar platter, a feast of stories.

Vicki Robin
Author, *Your Money or Your Life* and *Blessing the Hands That Feed Us: Lessons from a 10-Mile Diet*
May 2016

Introduction

"Our dream is that the community will feed itself.
The only question people will ask about their food is
which of their neighbors' farms it came from."
—Henning Sehmsdorf, S&S Homestead Farm

WELCOME TO THIS INTIMATE, behind-the-scenes view of what it takes to bring food from earth to table on Lopez Island, one of Washington State's San Juan Islands. This book, the result of a three-year, community-funded project supported in part by the Lopez Community Land Trust (LCLT) and Lopez Locavores, adds some new pages to the history of farming on Lopez Island. Here you'll find images and profiles of twenty-eight Lopez Island farms and the people who care for them, along with recipes using the bounty of the farmers' labor. You'll discover how today's farmers are revitalizing the tradition of feeding their community.

Farming and fishing have been a way of life on Lopez Island beginning with Native Americans who fished and hunted here 7,000 to 9,000 years ago. According to records from the Lopez Island Historical Society and Museum, Europeans arrived in the mid-1800s. Some early Lopez farmers were the sons and daughters of Irish farmers who fled the potato famine of the 1840s. Prospectors followed during the short-lived Fraser River Gold Rush, passing through the San Juan Islands on their way to and from unproductive goldfields.

Other settlers arrived from the Midwest (principally Iowa) and Canada. They raised cattle, sheep, pigs, and chickens as well as crops of fruit, vegetables, hay, and oats. Dairying was well developed, too, and by 1908, the island had its own creamery and shipped 1,500 pounds of butter a month to the mainland. By 1930, there were 134 farms on the island, producing food for local families as well as sending cream, eggs, poultry, and fruit off-island. Almost every farmer also fished, returning to the farm when the salmon run was over.

In 2013, Project Manager Sue Roundy conceived of BOUNTY as a way to use photographic art to recognize the abundance of fresh, healthy food grown and raised on Lopez Island today. In the project's first phase, local photographers Robert S. Harrison, Steve Horn, and Summer Moon Scriver photographed the farmers, their land, and the food they produce. Their stunning images premiered in October 2014 in a color slide show during the LCLT's annual Harvest Dinner; that show is now available in a DVD, with musical accompaniment by Lopez musician Stanley Greenthal.

Phase II of BOUNTY produced a photography exhibit that represents the diversity and beauty of farming on Lopez Island in these times. Lopez author Iris Graville wrote profiles to accompany the farmers' portraits. Those brief biographies, included here, reflect the farmers' responses to questions about why they farm, some of their greatest challenges and rewards, and the lessons they've learned as farmers. Perhaps most revealing are the three words the farmers use to describe what inspires them in their work.

The project's third phase is the book you're holding. In addition to the photographs and profiles, Lopez chef (and farmer at Windy Bottom Farm) Kim Bast offers recipes using products from each of the farms. Once again, the photographers (with the assistance of food stylist Rachel Graville) convey the art of food and cooking. Book designer Jane Jeszeck elegantly fit all the pieces together.

We encourage you to enjoy this collection from a variety of perspectives. First, thumb through the pages to take in the expanse of the photographs. "There's a lot of agriculture, both large- and small-scale, happening on Lopez that so many people don't know about," says Ken Akopiantz of Horse Drawn Farm. It's the BOUNTY team's hope that, collectively, these images help tell the Lopez food story and will encourage people to, as Ken says, "...participate in our Lopez food system, both as producers and consumers."

Then look again, spending time with the photographs of the individual farms and the accompanying portraits and profiles. As Todd Goldsmith and Diane Dear of T&D Farms suggest, BOUNTY offers "...a little insight into why we farmers chose to do what we do, and why we chose Lopez."

Finally, and perhaps most important, purchase some of the fruit, vegetables, meat, seafood, cheese, wine, and bread produced on this island of just under thirty square miles of land. Then, with the recipes in this book to inspire you, use this bounty to feed yourself, family, and friends.

This project would not have been possible without the support of the BOUNTY team, the farmers, volunteers, individual donors, Publishing Partners and Publishing Associates, and these organizations: Lopez Artists Guild, Lopez Community Land Trust, Lopez Locavores, and Lopez Thrift Shop. THANK YOU! Working together, BOUNTY is helping us again be a community that feeds itself and shares its abundance beyond its shores.

Chef Kim Bast

List of Recipes

color
camaraderie
soil

ARBORDOUN FARM
Susan Bill

FOR THIRTY YEARS, SUSAN BILL and her team of dedicated women have created floral abundance. They grow over fifty varieties of beautiful and unusual flowers and foliage, including showy spikes of Delphinium in purple, blue, and white; colorful lilies; unusual greens; golden sunflowers; and sweetly fragrant Freesia and Sweet Pea. Their flower arrangements have the reputation of being gorgeous and "on the wild side."

The women of Arbordoun also use many farm-grown herbs to produce Abundantly Herbal Calendula Cream and Silky Day Lotion. They pour these GMO–free cosmeceuticals into recyclable containers by hand and ship them throughout the country and beyond. Avid users write emphatic testimonials of the products' "salvation for aging skin" as well as "healing relief" for eczema, shingles, radiation burns, and many other skin challenges. "Our creams and lotions are edible herbals for working skin!"

Those Arbordoun herbs aren't the only edibles Susan raises. Every fall, espaliered apple trees bearing Akane, Jonagold, and Melrose varieties add their own color and fragrance to the farm.

"Growing flowers is my passion."

MAKES 1 QUART OF
APPLE MOLASSES TO USE
ALONE AND/OR TO MAKE
VINAIGRETTE AND PAN
SAUCE

MOLASSES

2 gallons freshly pressed,
    unfiltered apple cider, from
    either a single apple variety
    or a mix of varieties
A 12-quart or larger heavy
    bottomed, non-reactive
    stockpot
Clean jars for storage

VINAIGRETTE

1 small shallot, minced
½ cup sherry vinegar
1 heaping tablespoon Dijon
    mustard
2 to 3 tablespoons apple cider
    molasses (depending on
    tartness of molasses)
1½ to 2 cups olive oil
Kosher salt and freshly ground
    pepper to taste

PAN SAUCE

1 tablespoon finely chopped
    shallot
½ cup dry white wine
½ cup chicken stock
2 tablespoons apple cider
    molasses
1 teaspoon chopped fresh
    herbs (any combination that
    complements what the sauce
    is served with)
Kosher salt and ground pepper

apple cider molasses, vinaigrette, and pan sauce

MOLASSES

STEP 1 Bring apple cider to a boil over medium-high heat, stirring frequently
to make sure pot doesn't boil or foam over. Skim any foam from surface.

STEP 2 Reduce heat to medium-low to maintain a simmer. As cider thickens,
reduce heat to low. Continue reducing cider until it is the consistency of a
thick syrup that coats the back of a spoon (will be about 1 quart).

STEP 3 As it reduces, the molasses must be stirred often to avoid scorching.

STEP 4 Store apple cider molasses in an airtight container in the refrigerator
indefinitely.

VINAIGRETTE

STEP 1 In a stainless steel bowl, combine the shallot, sherry vinegar, Dijon
mustard, and apple cider molasses.

STEP 2 Gently stir in the oil with a whisk, ½ cup at a time, until desired taste
and consistency. Add salt and pepper to taste.

PAN SAUCE

STEP 1 Once your meat or poultry has finished cooking, remove to a warm
platter and tent with foil to rest.

STEP 2 Pour off all but 1 to 2 tablespoons of fat from the cooking pan,
retaining all juices and bits in pan.

STEP 3 Add chopped shallots to the cooking pan with the fat, and over
medium heat, sauté until translucent, about 1 minute.

STEP 4 Add the remaining ingredients to pan and bring to a gentle simmer,
stirring to remove any browned bits from the bottom of pan. Simmer until
sauce is the consistency of syrup. Salt and pepper to taste.

STEP 5 Remove sauce from heat and either dredge cooked meat in sauce or
drizzle sauce over meat before serving.

MOUNTAIN BREAD
$7

RYE, SPELT, OATS, FARRO,
FLAX, SESAME, SUNFLOWER,
PUMPKIN, MILLET, RAISINS,
YOGURT, BEER, HONEY
. . . . . .

form
function
love

all organic : whole grains
wild leavened : local
handmade : wood fired

Barn Owl
BAKERY

Midnight's Farm
Lopez Island WA
360-468-3492 : www.barnowlbakery.com

BARN OWL BAKERY
Sage Dilts and Nathan Hodges

BARN OWL, A 200-SQUARE-FOOT CRAFT BAKERY located on Midnight's Farm, produces breads and pastries following the oldest and simplest traditions. Sage Dilts and Nathan Hodges start with organic grain grown as close to Lopez as possible. The flours sit for a good part of a day, fermenting with wild yeasts and bacteria. The gently-worked dough rests, too—first in its bulk form and then as shaped loaves—for about ten hours while the bacteria acidify the dough and break down proteins (gluten).

The loaves bake in a wood-fired, vault style oven that Nathan built in the winter of 2013. It's heated with a mix of woods sourced locally from the scraps of woodworkers, arborists, and landscapers, as well as young woodlots that need thinning. On baking days, Nathan and Sage crank out crusty loaves of Country Miche, fragrant rosemary batards, and the Lopez Sandwich loaf, made with Lopez-grown and -milled Fortuna wheat. They're followed by scones, flat breads, cinnamon rolls, and cookies.

Everything Sage and Nathan put in their baked goods is organic, with local and seasonal ingredients as the priority. They use produce grown on Midnight's Farm, berries from Crowfoot Farm, and goat cheese from Sunnyfield Farm because, in their view, any savings from importing lower-priced foods are lost. "They'll never come around full circle as they do when we take the extra effort to sustain our local food economy."

> *"We make bread that's more than bread;*
> *we want our product to help shape a landscape*
> *that's healthier and that can sustain us."*

SERVES 4 AS MAIN DISH,
6 AS SIDE DISH

2½ pounds mixed, assorted,
 vine-ripened tomatoes,
 cut into 1-inch cubes

2 teaspoons kosher salt

6 generous cups cubed
 (1 inch), day-old, rustic
 bread, crusts removed

1 cup cooked dry beans such
 as cannellini (see Frances
 Kring Bean recipe, page 96,
 for instructions to cook dry
 beans)

1 small red onion, thinly sliced

2 stalks celery, finely diced

½ cup basil leaves, torn into
 small pieces

¼ cup shiso, or Italian parsley,
 leaves torn into small
 pieces

2 cloves garlic, crushed

2 tablespoons red wine
 vinegar

Freshly ground black pepper

½ cup best quality olive oil

Kosher salt to taste

panzanella salad with heirloom tomatoes, beans, basil, and shiso

STEP 1 In a colander set over a bowl, toss tomatoes with 2 teaspoons of salt. Set aside to drain for 15 minutes, tossing occasionally. Save collected tomato juice for vinaigrette.

STEP 2 Put the bread cubes in a serving bowl and sprinkle with enough cold water to dampen the bread. Let sit for a minute or two or until the bread is moist, but not soggy. Using your hands, gently break the bread into slightly smaller pieces and drain off any excess water.

STEP 3 Give tomatoes one last good shake to release any additional liquid and add them to the bread. Add beans, red onion, celery, basil, and shiso to bowl.

STEP 4 To the collected tomato juice, mix in the garlic, red wine vinegar, and black pepper to taste. Whisk in olive oil to combine.

STEP 5 Toss salad with vinaigrette, add salt to taste, and allow to stand for 30 minutes before serving to allow flavors to blend.

work at it

BUFFUM BROTHERS FARM
Gary Buffum and M.R. Buffum

BROTHERS GARY AND M.R. BUFFUM grew up on the farm they still work today. M.R. remembers buying his first Holstein bull calf when he was fifteen years old. Now, he and Gary work 1100 acres for grain, hay, pigs, and 130 calf/mother pairs (mostly Angus). When they're not taking care of their animals (or repairing fences), they're running another division of their farm—Lopez Sand & Gravel and Excavating. For decades, Gary and M.R. have worked in the islands clearing roads, building bulkheads, excavating ponds, logging, and delivering sand and gravel as well as wood chips, manure, and topsoil. Their advice for other farmers: "Don't spend money you don't have."

"Fences are the biggest challenge.
You just get through building or fixing one,
and you start over again."

NUOC CHAM SAUCE

¼ cup fresh lime juice

5 tablespoons fish sauce

6 tablespoons water

3 tablespoons sugar

1 large clove garlic, finely
chopped

1 fresh Thai, Bird, or Serrano
chili pepper, cut in half,
seeded, and thinly sliced,
or 1 teaspoon chili flakes

PEANUT SAUCE

¾ cup unsweetened peanut
butter (natural-style,
creamy, or chunky)

2 cloves garlic, finely minced

2 scant tablespoons tamarind
pulp dissolved in 2
tablespoons warm water
(discard any solids) or
substitute 2 tablespoons
fresh lime juice

2 tablespoons fresh lime
juice (in addition to 2
tablespoons above if used
to substitute for tamarind
pulp)

1½ tablespoons soy sauce,
more to taste

1½ tablespoons hoisin sauce

Water for thinning sauce

1 fresh Thai, Bird, or Serrano
chili pepper, cut in half,
seeded, and finely minced,
or 1 teaspoon chili flakes

lettuce wraps with ground beef and two sauces

NUOC CHAM SAUCE

STEP 1 In a small bowl, mix lime juice, fish sauce, water, and sugar, until sugar dissolves.

STEP 2 Stir in garlic and chili pepper, and set aside.

PEANUT SAUCE

STEP 1 In a medium bowl, mix peanut butter, garlic, tamarind pulp, lime juice, soy sauce, and hoisin sauce.

STEP 2 Whisk ¼ to ½ cup water into the sauce until the sauce is thick, yet pourable, but not runny.

STEP 3 Stir in chili pepper, taste, and if desired, adjust saltiness with more soy sauce. Set aside.

WRAPS

2 tablespoons organic peanut
  oil
1 rounded tablespoon finely
  chopped ginger
1 rounded tablespoon finely
  chopped garlic
1 pound ground beef
2 tablespoons soy sauce
1 tablespoon fish sauce
2 teaspoons light brown sugar
1 head of bibb lettuce,
  washed, with whole leaves
  separated
2 carrots, cut into thin
  matchsticks, or grated
1 English cucumber, cut into
  thin matchsticks
1 bunch green onions, cut on
  the diagonal into thin slices
1 cup cilantro leaves

WRAPS

STEP 1 In a skillet over high heat, heat peanut oil until it glistens. Add garlic and ginger and cook, stirring constantly, until fragrant, about 30 seconds.

STEP 2 Add ground beef to the pan and cook, using a spoon to break up the beef and pressing it down firmly to encourage browning, until it is almost cooked through, about 5 minutes.

STEP 3 While stirring constantly, add soy sauce, fish sauce, and brown sugar.

STEP 4 Continue to cook and stir beef until all of the liquid has evaporated from the pan, about 2 more minutes. Remove from heat.

STEP 5 To serve wraps, place 2 to 4 tablespoons of beef into the cup of the whole lettuce leaves. Sprinkle beef with grated carrot, cucumbers, green onion, and a few cilantro leaves, and serve with prepared dipping sauces.

tradition

nutrition

regeneration

CHICKADEE PRODUCE
Clarissa and Charles Mish

CHARLES MISH GREW UP IN MICHIGAN around aunts and uncles who raised vegetables, chickens, and pigs and operated a cheese factory. Seeing their direct connection with nature made an impression on him: "It's what I wanted to recapture when Clarissa and I started growing our own food." The couple views their biodynamic farm as a way to help with climate change and regenerate the earth. "With more organic farming," Charles says, "we could actually begin to reverse global warming by sequestering carbon dioxide in the living soil."

On the farm, Charles strives for the right balance of manure, compost, and sea crop trace minerals to enrich the soil, while also combating quack grass and slugs. The payoff? "Food that doesn't taste like cardboard."

Chickadee Produce includes fruit (Spartan, Jonagold, Melrose, Red Gravenstein, and Brown Russet apples; Asian and Bosc pears; and Mirabelle plums) and potatoes. People tell Charles they can taste the quality with his Yukon Gold, German Butterball, Yellow Finn, and Nicola potatoes. His favorites are the French Fingerlings. "Sliced, cooked in olive oil, and seasoned with a sprig of rosemary . . . " Charles says, "delicious."

"All across America, industrial agriculture is sterilizing our topsoil, devitalizing our food, and warming the planet. We grow GMO-free, nutrient-dense food to nourish our family and our customers who crave real food."

1 pound fresh pears, peeled, cored, and cut into 1-inch pieces

1 pound dried figs, quartered

2 cups good-quality apple cider vinegar

2 tablespoons local honey

3 tablespoons brown mustard seeds

2 sticks whole cinnamon stick

1 teaspoon coarsely ground black pepper

Clean jars for storing

An assortment of locally-sourced cheeses: aged, rind ripened, and fresh

pear and fig mostarda with local cheeses

STEP 1 Lightly toast mustard seeds in a small skillet over medium heat. When the seeds begin to pop, cover the skillet and immediately remove from the heat.

STEP 2 Combine all ingredients in a non-reactive saucepan. Bring to a gentle simmer over medium to medium-low heat and stir frequently to prevent scorching. Cook until the majority of the liquid has evaporated and the dried figs are soft but not unrecognizable.

STEP 3 Remove from the heat and discard the cinnamon sticks. Allow to cool completely before placing in storage jars. Mostarda will keep in the refrigerator for up to one month.

STEP 4 Serve as a condiment on a charcuterie board with an assortment of cheeses.

Tristar

Albion
(the big ones)

nature

taste

pleasure

Pick strawberries into a bucket or a flat. A bucket is easier for large quantities and/or large groups. Picking directly into a flat keeps the berries in better shape.

Strawb's cost $4./lb. and ⅓ of a bucket is about $13.

CROWFOOT FARM
Eric Hall and Elf Fay

AS A YOUNG COUPLE, ELF FAY AND ERIC HALL wanted a lifestyle that integrated their home-life and their work with their values. They find pleasure in doing work that is basic and essential, and Crowfoot Farm fulfilled their lifelong dream of growing fruit and working outdoors. Their certified organic farm, which sells strawberries, raspberries, and blueberries, has become a Lopez institution. Both locals and off-islanders express that they love getting great berries and sharing in the beauty and vision of what Eric and Elf have created.

An interconnectedness with nature is the couple's greatest joy and their biggest challenge. "We can work hard and do everything right and still lose most of our crop to rain. There's nothing more depressing than a field of moldy strawberries!"

"The berries and the weather are part of a natural system.
While we can influence it, we can't be sure
of a particular outcome. We are not in control."

MAKES A 9- OR 10-INCH
PIE

Butter (to butter pie plate)
½ cup unsalted butter, at
    room temperature
¼ cup light brown sugar
⅓ cup finely ground pecans
1 cup all-purpose flour
4 pints freshly picked
    strawberries
¾ cup water
2 tablespoons orange liqueur
    such as Grand Marnier or
    Cointreau (optional)
½ cup sugar
2½ tablespoons cornstarch
Whipped cream for garnish
    (optional)

fresh strawberry pie

The pie is equally delicious when made with fresh raspberries.

STEP 1 Butter the sides and bottom of a 9- or 10-inch pie plate and preheat oven to 350°.

STEP 2 In a mixing bowl, beat together the butter and brown sugar until light and creamy, about 30 seconds.

STEP 3 Add finely ground pecans and flour and mix until well combined.

STEP 4 Using buttered fingers, press crust into buttered pie plate, on the bottom and up sides in an even layer. If you'd like, press tines of a fork into edge of the crust to decorate.

STEP 5 Bake the unfilled pie crust for 15 to 20 minutes, or until pale gold in color. Remove from oven and cool.

STEP 6 In the bowl of a food processor, mash 1 pint of strawberries.

STEP 7 In a saucepan over medium-high heat, combine mashed strawberries, orange liqueur, water, sugar, and cornstarch. Stir constantly as glaze comes to a boil, thickens, and becomes shiny. Remove from heat and cool until warm to the touch and still spreadable.

STEP 8 Depending on the size of your strawberries, slice, or halve, 3 pints of berries. Mound sliced berries into pre-baked pie shell.

STEP 9 Pour warm glaze over top of berries, using a spatula to distribute evenly, and smooth.

STEP 10 Chill for at least 2 hours before serving with optional whipped cream.

soggy sheep
frolicking lambs

FLINT BEACH OHANA
Sally and Tom Reeve

ALTHOUGH SALLY REEVE WAS FAMILIAR with corn and soybean farming while growing up in southern Indiana, she never imagined raising sheep or chickens. And her husband, Tom, had no connection to farming until they "inherited" some North Country Cheviot sheep when they bought their land near Iceberg Point. They soon discovered this breed has a tendency to roam. "They'd get around the fence and clamber on the beach and up the cliffs," Tom says.

Sheep farmers Oakley Goodner and Becky and Dave Heinlein offered guidance and steered the couple to books about managing ewes and lambs. Sally would read in the barn late at night by flashlight, with a cat on her lap, learning how to care for sheep in, as she says, "a non-chemical, non-mass production mode." Eventually, Sally realized that caring for her flock and juggling numerous other commitments (such as being an EMT with Lopez Fire Department) was more than she could handle alone. With the assistance of Dave Rucker, Sally experimented with a variety of breeds and now offers pasture-raised, USDA-inspected Romney lamb, with the "essence of salt spray from the Straits." The farm also sells eggs in shades from light brown to blueish, all with deep orange yolks.

"The patterns in farming, whether it be the seasonality of activities or the processes, give one a satisfying sense of time and place."

SERVES 6

1 large yellow onion

4 cloves garlic, finely chopped

2 tablespoons kosher salt

1 3½- to 4½-pound leg of
   lamb, boned and butterflied

2 cups plain, whole milk
   yogurt

1 cup mint leaves, coarsely
   chopped

1 cup parsley, leaves and
   stems, coarsely chopped

1 teaspoon ground cumin

1 teaspoon freshly ground
   black pepper

Butcher's twine for tying leg
   of lamb

slow-roasted butterflied leg of lamb with yogurt, mint, and parsley

STEP 1 Coarsely grate onion in a food processor, or on a box grater over a dish, to capture all onion juice. Mix grated onion and onion juice with chopped garlic and salt.

STEP 2 If the leg of lamb is tied up or in a mesh bag, remove it. In a shallow bowl or baking dish, coat all sides of lamb leg with onion mixture, cover, and refrigerate overnight, turning the lamb at least once while it marinates.

STEP 3 In a medium bowl, mix together yogurt, mint, parsley, ground cumin, and black pepper. Refrigerate overnight, or at least a few hours, to let flavors mingle.

STEP 4 About an hour before roasting, remove lamb and yogurt mixture from refrigerator. Coat lamb evenly with yogurt mixture, return to marinating dish, and let stand at room temperature for an hour.

STEP 5 Preheat oven to 450°.

STEP 6 Roll the leg of lamb, keeping the de-boned side on the inside of your roll, into a rough cylinder.

STEP 7 On a cutting board, place 3 pieces of butcher's twine, each 18 inches long, horizontally, 3 to 4 inches apart. Lay the rolled lamb leg, rolled edge tucked underneath, perpendicular to, and in the middle of the pieces of butcher's twine. Starting with the middle piece of twine, tie a secure knot around the center of the lamb leg to keep it together. Repeat with upper and lower pieces of twine, and trim any excess twine.

STEP 8 Place the rolled lamb leg on a rack in an oiled, shallow baking dish. Slather a few tablespoons of marinade over the leg before placing it in the oven.

STEP 9 Immediately reduce oven temperature to 250° and slow-roast lamb until an instant-read thermometer placed in the middle of the leg reads 125° to 135°, about 1 to 1½ hours.

STEP 10 Remove lamb from oven, tent with foil, and let rest for 15 to 20 minutes. Remove strings, and slice lamb thinly, against the grain of the meat.

life
work
gratitude

HELEN'S FARM
Julie and Blake Johnston

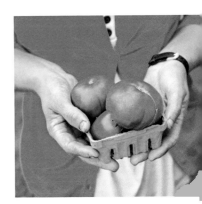

JULIE AND BLAKE JOHNSTON HAVE OVERCOME one of the most difficult challenges facing aspiring Lopez farmers—finding land. After honing their skills at S & S Homestead Farm, they dreamed of starting Helen's Farm, named after two Helens—Julie's grandmother (who was a farmer) and Blake's great-grandmother. For a few years, they leased a half-dozen small parcels scattered across the island to raise organic vegetables, broiler chickens, pigs, and grass-fed cattle. Now they've consolidated their farming efforts, leasing 50 acres from Rita O'Boyle in the center of the island. On this land that had for many years been harvested for hay, Blake and Julie are trying "to help our little corner of the world function in a thoughtful and healthy way." They strive to strike a balance between developing an efficient and productive farm without depleting resources that they know are in short supply. Farming is teaching them to take things slowly—allowing themselves "to develop, grow, and change" in ways they hadn't expected.

"Farming provides us a connection with our past.
It's beautiful, fascinating, physical work,
always new and challenging."

SERVES 6

BRINE

2 teaspoons whole coriander

1 tablespoon whole black
  peppercorns

⅔ cup kosher salt

⅓ cup light brown sugar

1 large lemon, zest finely
  grated on a microplane
  (no pith), and lemon
  reserved for roasting

1 teaspoon Spanish smoked
  paprika

1 teaspoon Hungarian sharp
  paprika, or plain paprika
  plus a pinch of ground
  cayenne pepper

2 bay leaves

6 slightly heaping cups
  ice cubes

Paper towels to dry chicken

One 4- to 4½-pound roasting
  chicken, preferably sourced
  locally and pasture-raised

RUB

1 teaspoon whole coriander

1 teaspoon whole black
  peppercorns

2 teaspoons Spanish smoked
  paprika

1 teaspoon Hungarian sharp
  paprika, or plain paprika
  plus a pinch of ground
  cayenne pepper

1 teaspoon kosher salt

brined and roasted chicken with smoked paprika and lemon

STEP 1 Toast whole coriander and whole black peppercorns (for both the brine and the rub) in a small dry skillet over medium heat, shaking often until fragrant, about 3 to 5 minutes. Set aside to cool. Roughly crush coriander and peppercorns separately in a mortar and pestle or spice grinder. For the brine you'll need 2 scant teaspoons of ground coriander and 1 scant tablespoon ground black pepper. Set aside 1 scant teaspoon of each for the rub (see step 9).

STEP 2 In a 2-quart saucepan, over medium-high heat, dissolve kosher salt and light brown sugar in 2 cups of water. Bring brine base to full simmer, stirring often, making sure that all sugar and salt are dissolved.

STEP 3 To brine base, add crushed coriander and black pepper, lemon zest, Spanish smoked and Hungarian sharp paprikas, and bay leaves. Simmer for 1 minute. Remove from heat and cool for 30 minutes.

STEP 4 Place ice cubes in a bowl just large enough to hold the chicken and accommodate the brine.

STEP 5 Pour brine over ice cubes and add 4 cups cold water. Mix well to cool brine and distribute spices and salt. Brine should be cold when chicken is added.

STEP 6 Place the chicken in the bowl with the brine, making sure that brine fills the interior cavity of the chicken, and the chicken is covered with the brine. Add more water if necessary, mixing well to incorporate. Soak chicken in brine for 3 to 4 hours in the refrigerator.

STEP 7 Remove chicken from brine, and place on a wire rack over a rimmed sheet pan. Discard brine.

STEP 8 Using paper towels, thoroughly dry off exterior and interior of chicken.

STEP 9 In a small bowl, combine all ingredients for the rub and mix well. Evenly sprinkle the rub all over the outside of the chicken, rubbing it in if necessary to get it to stick to the surface of the chicken.

STEP 10 Return chicken to refrigerator, uncovered, for 30 to 60 minutes.

STEP 11 Remove chicken from the refrigerator and let it rest on the counter for 30 to 45 minutes. While the chicken rests, preheat oven to 425°.

STEP 12 Drizzle olive oil over all surfaces of the chicken. Cut reserved lemon in half and place both halves inside the chicken. Place chicken, breast side up, on wire rack placed over a rimmed sheet pan, and bake in the middle of the oven for 20 minutes, or until breast is golden brown.

1 large lemon, zest finely grated
    on a microplane (no pith)

1 teaspoon fresh thyme leaves

2 to 3 tablespoons olive oil

STEP 13   Reduce oven temperature to 350°, flip chicken over so that the breast side is down, and bake for 30 minutes or until back side is golden brown.

STEP 14   Flip chicken once more, breast side up, and roast until an instant-read thermometer inserted into the thigh meat registers 160°. Remove chicken from the oven, tent with foil, and allow it to rest for 10 to 15 minutes before carving.

STEP 15   Place chicken on a cutting board, remove lemons from interior cavity, and set aside.

STEP 16   Cut the legs off of the chicken, leaving legs whole or separating drumsticks from thighs, and place on a warm serving platter. Remove wings to platter. Carve the breast meat or separate the whole breasts (ribs attached) from the chicken, cut each in half, and add to the platter.

STEP 17   Squeeze both halves of the cooked lemon over the chicken and serve.

FARMSTAND

welcome

HORSE DRAWN FARM

FARMSTAND

HORSE DRAWN PRODUCE

LOCAL ORGANICALLY GROWN

beauty
abundance
cycles

yum

HORSE DRAWN FARM
Ken Akopiantz and Kathryn Thomas

NOTHING GOES TO WASTE at Horse Drawn's 80-acre farm along Port Stanley Road. For example, the pigs that Kathryn Thomas and Ken Akopiantz raise eat the "cull" vegetables (organic and delicious, just not pretty), and their bedding and manure turns into fertilizer. The chickens eat all the family's household food waste. Ken and Kathryn apply these and other sustainable practices to raise vegetables, herbs, flowers, cattle, Coopworth and North Country Cheviot sheep, and Berkshire/Hampshire pigs on their animal-powered (horses and oxen) farm. Horse Drawn products are available at a self-serve farm stand, open day and night, all year long. These long-time farmers can't imagine doing any other kind of work, and they view all the cycles, all the aspects of farming, as part of a big circle. They have some disappointments every year— plants that don't work, geese overrunning the fields, stillbirths with the animals, pests. "But we just keep going," they say. "We're rewarded by seeing people discover fresh food and knowing that ninety percent of what we raise is consumed locally."

"It's gratifying to raise food that's healthy and that sustains people and the land."

HALF LEG SERVES 8
TO 10, WHOLE LEG
SERVES 14 TO 16

One 8- to 10-pound, butt-
end, bone-in, leg of pork
roast, or one whole 15- to
20-pound, bone-in leg of
pork

½ cup fresh rosemary, finely
chopped by hand or pulsed
in a food processor/spice
grinder

6 cloves of garlic, finely
chopped by hand, or pulsed
in a food processor/spice
grinder

¼ cup Dijon mustard

¼ cup olive oil

2 tablespoons white wine

1 tablespoon kosher salt

1 tablespoon freshly ground
white pepper

1 tablespoon freshly ground
black pepper

roast leg of pork (fresh ham)

If cooking a whole 15- to 20-pound leg of pork, double the quantities for the rub, maintain the baking time at 450°, and double the cooking time at 325°.

STEP 1 Preheat oven to 450°.

STEP 2 Using a sharp knife, score the fat on the outside of the leg roast in a crisscross diamond pattern, making cuts about 1 inch apart. Be sure to only cut through the fat layer and not into the meat.

STEP 3 In a small bowl, combine the rosemary, garlic, Dijon mustard, olive oil, white wine, salt, white pepper, and black pepper. Mix well to emulsify the liquid ingredients in the rub.

STEP 4 Slather the rub all over the pork roast and place the roast, fat side up, on a rack in a shallow roasting pan. Place the roasting pan in the lower half of the oven.

STEP 5 After 20 minutes, lower the oven temperature to 325°.

STEP 6 Continue to roast until an instant-read thermometer inserted into the meat, not next to the bone, reads 145°, about 2 hours.

STEP 7 Remove roast from oven and tent with foil. Allow roast to rest for 20 to 30 minutes before carving to raise the internal temperature to 155° and redistribute the juices.

birds
bees
butterflies

J & M OCCASIONAL FRUIT
Margaret and Jim Birkemeier

JIM BIRKEMEIER HAS BEEN FARMING his entire life; as a boy, he hand-harvested hazelnuts from his family's orchard. Since the 1960s, he and Margaret have sustained an 80-acre organic hazelnut farm in Oregon; their daughter and son-in-law oversee that operation now. Here on Lopez, Jim follows the same philosophy of working with nature, rather than fighting it, to grow organic fruit—apples, Asian pears, blueberries, nectarines, and peaches. In his view, the main advantage of an organic system is that all the organisms are helping each other. "I look at the trees and the soil and figure out what would be best for them. Everything out there is there for a purpose," Jim says, even his biggest challenge, "the slugs and fungus. It's all interrelated, and it's amazing." Jim also believes that we all play an integral part in taking care of the planet. "How we live and relate to nature is how we develop spiritually."

"What are we most proud of in our work? A ripe peach."

MAKES A 9"X 9" CAKE

CAKE

4 tablespoons unsalted butter, softened

¾ cup sugar

2 cups all purpose flour

2½ teaspoons baking powder

¼ teaspoon salt

¾ cup milk

1 egg

2 cups fresh blueberries

CRUMB TOPPING

½ cup sugar

⅓ cup all purpose flour

½ teaspoon cinnamon

4 tablespoons unsalted butter, room temperature

MAKES 2½ CUPS

2 large egg yolks

¼ cup + 1 tablespoon sugar

3 tablespoons lemon juice, freshly squeezed

2 tablespoon unsalted butter, softened

1 teaspoon lemon zest, finely shredded

1 cup whipping cream

1 tablespoon sugar

blueberry buckle with lemon curd whipped cream

STEP 1 Preheat oven to 375° and butter cake pan.

STEP 2 For crumb topping, combine flour, cinnamon, and sugar. Using two forks, or a pastry knife, cut room temperature butter into dry ingredients to form pea-sized crumbs. Set aside.

STEP 3 Combine flour, salt, and baking powder in small bowl. Combine lightly beaten egg and milk.

STEP 4 Cream butter and sugar in a mixing bowl until light and fluffy. Add half of dry mixture and half of milk-egg mixture, beating at medium speed for about 20 seconds. Scrape down sides and bottom of bowl and repeat with remaining ingredients.

STEP 5 The cake batter will be very stiff. Using a rubber spatula, gently fold blueberries into batter.

STEP 6 Scrape into prepared baking dish, spreading batter into pan evenly. Sprinkle crumb topping on top of cake batter.

STEP 7 Bake cake in the center of the oven for 45 to 50 minutes, or until cake tester poked half-way between side and center of cake comes out clean.

STEP 8 Allow cake to cool for at least an hour before serving. Serve each piece with a generous dollop of Lemon Curd Whipped Cream (recipe follows).

lemon curd whipped cream

STEP 1 In a small, heavy bottomed, stainless steel saucepan (do not use an aluminum pan) beat sugar and egg yolks until thoroughly combined. Add lemon juice and butter.

STEP 2 Cook curd over medium-low heat, stirring constantly, until foam subsides, the color turns opaque, and the curd thickens to coat the back of the spoon. Do not let the curd boil or it will curdle.

STEP 3 Pour through a fine-meshed sieve to remove any coagulated bits of egg. Mix in lemon zest and cool completely.

STEP 4 Beat whipping cream and sugar in a chilled bowl until mixture slightly thickens but before any peaks appear.

STEP 5 Add chilled lemon curd and beat until stiff peaks form.

family
passion
persistence

JONES FAMILY FARM

Sara and Nick Jones

PRODUCING FOOD AND RESTORING FARMLAND has become a family mission for Jones Family Farm. "As much as we work," Nick Jones says, "we're together, and that's contributed to our closeness and success as a family." To achieve their goals, much of the family's work involves creating good grass in the fields for their mixed breed cattle that are slaughtered on the farm and then dry-aged for at least two weeks. Hampshire hogs are an integral part of the farm's grazing- and pasture-management program, too. The hogs are raised free-range on diverse pasture where they eat forage grasses, plant roots, and bugs and grubs from the soil. Jones Family Farm's sheep and heritage breed goats are also free-range and grass-pastured, with their feed supplemented with Lopez-grown organic grains. In addition to meats and grain, the farm also grows produce and flowers. For Sara and Nick, much of their satisfaction, though, "comes from the relationships we've developed with landowners, business partners, suppliers, employees, and customers."

"To feed and employ people, and to make the lands, beaches, and pastures of the island that have been idle, productive, is a creative process in service to the world."

SERVES 6

TACOS

1 teaspoon ground cumin

½ teaspoon ground coriander

1 teaspoon chopped fresh
  oregano, or ½ teaspoon
  dried oregano

1½ teaspoons kosher salt

½ teaspoon freshly ground
  black pepper

2- to 3-pound goat-neck
  steaks, or goat shoulder
  or goat leg cut into 2-inch
  chunks

1 tablespoon lard or olive oil

1 cup chopped onions

3 cloves garlic, peeled, and
  smashed with the side of a
  chef's knife

1 bay leaf

2 cups chicken stock or water

1½ cups milk

½ cup orange juice

12 to 15 homemade, or best
  quality, store-bought corn
  tortillas

1 red onion, quartered
  vertically, and thinly sliced

½ cup apple cider vinegar

1 teaspoon sugar

1 teaspoon kosher salt

1 bunch radishes, thinly sliced

1 cup cilantro leaves

3 cups thinly sliced cabbage

2 limes, cut into wedges

carnitas-style goat tacos with pickled onions and salsa roja

STEP 1 In a small bowl, combine cumin, coriander, oregano, salt, and black pepper. Rub spice mixture all over the meat.

STEP 2 Heat lard, or olive oil, over high heat, in a Dutch oven or heavy-bottomed pot, large enough to hold the meat in a single layer.

STEP 3 Add meat and brown on all sides, in batches if necessary, about 5 to 7 minutes.

STEP 4 Reduce heat to medium, add onions and garlic, and cook, stirring often, until soft, about 5 minutes.

STEP 5 Add the bay leaf, broth or water, and bring to a simmer. Use a spoon to scrape any brown bits from the bottom of the Dutch oven or pot.

STEP 6 Cover, and reduce heat to low, just enough to maintain a gentle simmer. Cook about 1 hour, until goat is fork tender.

STEP 7 Pour off all cooking liquids (save for making beans or rice), and add milk and orange juice to the meat.

STEP 8 Bring to a simmer over medium heat, reduce heat to medium-low, and cook, stirring often as the liquids evaporate, to make sure the meat doesn't burn on the bottom of the pot.

STEP 9 All liquids will evaporate and goat meat will be nicely browned, about 45 minutes to 1 hour. Before serving, remove any bones and coarsely chop or shred meat.

STEP 10 While meat cooks, make salsa (recipe follows), and pickle red onions and warm tortillas (see step 11).

STEP 11 Combine red onion, cider vinegar, sugar, and salt in a small bowl. Allow the onions to sit at room temperature to pickle for 1 hour before serving. Wrap tortillas in aluminum foil and warm in a 350° oven for 15 to 20 minutes before serving.

STEP 12 Arrange taco condiments (pickled onions, sliced radishes, cilantro, sliced cabbage, and lime wedges) on a large serving platter, wrap warm tortillas in a cloth kitchen towel, and allow guests to make their own tacos. Serve with bowls of Salsa Roja.

MAKES 1 CUP

SALSA

10 dried guajillos, pasillas, or
    ancho chile peppers

1 large, ripe tomato

1 medium white onion,
    peeled and sliced into
    1-inch rounds

3 cloves garlic, peeled

¼ cup water

1 teaspoon kosher salt

1 cup finely chopped cilantro

salsa roja

STEP 1 Preheat a cast iron skillet over medium heat. Dry roast (no oil) chiles on both sides in hot skillet, using a spatula to press them against the hot skillet, until color changes slightly, about 1 to 2 minutes. Remove from skillet.

STEP 2 Increase heat under skillet to medium-high, and dry roast (no oil) onion rounds, garlic cloves, and whole tomato until slightly charred and blackened on all sides, about 3 to 5 minutes. Remove from skillet.

STEP 3 Once chiles are cool enough to handle, remove and discard tops and seeds.

STEP 4 In a blender or bowl of a food processor, purée the toasted chiles, tomato, onion rounds, garlic cloves, water, and salt. Stir in chopped cilantro by hand and taste for salt.

Sunflower Family
Compositae (Asteraceae)
Artichoke, cardoon, endive, Jerusalem
artichoke, lettuce, salsify, sunflower,
yacon

Goosefoot Family
Chenopodiaceae
Amaranth, beet, chard, huauzontle,
lamb's quarters, orach, quinoa,
spinach

Mustard Family
Brassicaceae (Cruciferae)
Broccoli, Brussel sprouts, cabbage,
cauliflower, Chinese cabbage,
collards, horseradish, kale, kohlrabi,
mustard, radish, rhutabaga, turnip

Lily Family
Amarylidaceae (Liliaceae)
Chives, Garlic, leek, onion

resilience
self-reliance
sharing

LOPEZ COMMUNITY LAND TRUST SEED LIBRARY

Ken Akopiantz, Seed Librarian

EVERYONE KNOWS ABOUT BORROWING BOOKS from a library, but on Lopez Island, gardeners and farmers can borrow—and return—seeds at the Lopez Community Land Trust (LCLT) Seed Library. The LCLT developed this community seed project to preserve and develop open-pollinated seeds suited to the island's unique maritime climate. The Seed Library, located next to the LCLT office at the Common Ground neighborhood, is a temperature- and humidity-controlled vault that provides a safe and organized place to store seeds.

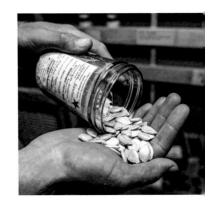

Seed Librarian (and farmer) Ken Akopiantz developed a Seed Exchange Catalog that lists everything from beans to turnips, with many varieties named in honor of local residents. Among the seeds you'll find in the catalog are island heirloom beans such as the Bond Bean, from Joe Bond of Orcas Island, and the Kring Bean, from Frances Kring of Lopez. Steven's Kabocha squash, grown and bred by Lopezian Steven Wrubleski, "is destined to become an heirloom," and Fortuna Wheat, introduced on Lopez in 2008, is regularly used by Barn Owl Bakery to create its "Lopez Loaf."

"The basic idea is—you plant the seeds,
let some go to seed, then return
some of these next generation seeds
for others to borrow."

potato, celeriac, and fennel gratin

MAKES ONE SHALLOW 2-QUART GRATIN (4 TO 6 SERVINGS)

- 1½ pounds firm-fleshed potatoes, scrubbed and thinly sliced
- ½ of a large celeriac (celery root), scrubbed, peeled, and thinly sliced
- 1 large fennel bulb, cored and thinly sliced
- 1 clove of garlic, peeled and cut in half lengthwise
- 1 tablespoon butter
- 2 cups freshly grated cheese: Swiss, Gruyère, Emmental, or Comté
- 1½ cups whole milk
- ½ cup heavy cream
- 1 teaspoon fresh thyme
- Kosher salt and freshly ground black pepper to taste

STEP 1 Preheat oven to 375°. Rub inside of baking dish with garlic. Butter sides and bottom of baking dish.

STEP 2 Combine 1½ cups of grated cheese, milk, cream, and thyme. Add salt and pepper to taste.

STEP 3 Pour enough of the cheese and milk mixture into the baking dish to evenly coat bottom of dish.

STEP 4 Tile vegetables into the dish by starting at one end of baking dish with a row or two of potatoes, followed by a row of celeriac, and finishing with a row of fennel. Repeat until all vegetables are used and you have filled the baking dish.

STEP 5 Pour the remainder of cheese and milk mixture over vegetables in baking dish, making sure liquid penetrates all vegetable layers evenly.

STEP 6 Top with the remaining ½ cup of cheese and a few grinds of black pepper. Place baking dish on a rimmed cookie sheet in case it bubbles over while baking. Bake for 1 hour and 15 minutes or until all vegetables are fork tender and the gratin is bubbling, crisp, and golden brown on top.

beauty
flavor
community

LOPEZ HARVEST
Christine Langley

FOR CHRISTINE LANGLEY, farming has been her life, her living, and her livelihood for over half of the years she's been alive. She loves to be outside and get dirty, both of which she does to raise organic salad greens, herbs, and other produce. Farming isn't a static picture for Christine—it's a process, with challenges and rewards that are the foundation of her daily life and commitment to sustainable land stewardship. "We don't have much rich farmland for row crops on Lopez," she says, "so most of us are in a constant dance to balance income-producing crops with inputs to improve the soil and, therefore, the harvest." Some days Christine revels in the "chaotic places" on the farm where her plantings of lupines, crimson clover, and many other "non-crop" plants naturalize with local weeds to create environments where pollinators and other beneficial insects thrive. Other days, she celebrates planting into soil that started out rather thin, but after years of cultivation with compost and cover crops, is much improved. "Gratifying too," she says, "are the times a customer expresses enthusiastic appreciation for the fruits of my labor."

"In farming, as in life, challenges and lessons
are two sides of the same coin."

SERVES 6

SALAD

1 medium red onion, quartered lengthwise, and cut into ¼-inch slices

½ cup unfiltered apple cider vinegar

1 teaspoon sugar

1 teaspoon kosher salt

2 bunches kale or mustard greens, about 1½ pounds

¼ cup blackberry vinegar (see recipe below), other berry vinegar, or apple cider vinegar

1 teaspoon coarse sea salt, or 1 scant teaspoon kosher salt

1 cup whole toasted almonds, roughly chopped

1 bunch radishes, thinly sliced

2 to 4 tablespoons olive oil

MAKES 2 CUPS

VINEGAR

2 cups blackberries

2 cups unfiltered apple cider vinegar

wilted over-wintered greens salad with blackberry vinegar and pickled red onion

Most years, our Pacific Maritime climate allows us to grow hearty greens throughout the winter. In early spring, as the days get longer, the plants produce an abundance of tender leaves and shoots.

STEP 1 Combine red onion, ½ cup apple cider vinegar, sugar, and salt in a small bowl. Set aside at room temperature for 1 hour.

STEP 2 If kale/mustard greens are young and tender, cut the leaves into 1-inch ribbons and stems into 1-inch pieces. If leaves are large and stems woody, discard stems and cut leaves in half before cutting into 1-inch ribbons.

STEP 3 In a large bowl, sprinkle coarse sea salt or kosher salt over greens. Using metal tongs, vigorously beat the kale leaves against the side of the bowl. Once the leaves begin to wilt, about 1 to 2 minutes, add blackberry vinegar, and continue to work greens for 1 to 2 more minutes. Set greens aside at room temperature, stirring occasionally, for 30 to 60 minutes. The volume of the greens will decrease by almost half.

STEP 4 Drain onions and add to wilted greens. Add radishes and almonds, and toss to combine.

STEP 5 Drizzle 2 tablespoons of olive oil on salad and toss, adding more if needed, to evenly coat greens.

blackberry vinegar

STEP 1 In a quart jar, mash the blackberries with a fork.

STEP 2 In a small saucepan over medium-high heat, bring the vinegar to a gentle simmer. Remove from heat and pour over mashed blackberries.

STEP 3 Allow the mixture to steep in a cool, dark place, covered, for 7 to 10 days.

STEP 4 Strain out solids and discard. Store blackberry vinegar in the refrigerator for up to 3 months.

lambs
loyal customers
spring

LOPEZ ISLAND FARM
Bruce Dunlop and Debbie Young

WHEN BRUCE DUNLOP BOUGHT THE LAND that became Lopez Island Farm, he was drawn most to its beauty. But, since he owned farmland, he thought it would be a shame to not use it. He's not fond of weeding, so he knew that "raising vegetables was out." Instead, he and Debbie work their land for pasture-raised pork and grass-fed lamb. Their system of rotational grazing for both the pigs and sheep continually improves the fertility of the soil and the vigor of forage growth. "It also results in healthy animals," Bruce says. "Our pigs get vitamins and minerals from grazing green plants and exercise from rooting in the ground."

Bruce also provided leadership with the Lopez Community Land Trust to design and develop the nation's first USDA-inspected Mobile Processing Unit. Now owned and operated by Island Grown Farmers Cooperative, the unit makes it possible for Bruce, as well as many farmers on Lopez and throughout the region, to slaughter and process animals in the field. "This reduces for animals the stresses associated with transporting and processing in commercial slaughterhouses," Bruce says. Thirteen similar units operate in North America now, and Bruce serves as a consultant to other communities interested in them.

"Every year you get to try again, to keep tweaking.
There's always something more to learn
or something new to try."

LAMB SHANKS

5 pounds lamb shanks (4 to 6
shanks), sawed into 2-inch
slices or cut to the bone
every 2 inches

¼ cup olive oil + 2 tablespoons
for sautéing

4 teaspoons ground cinnamon

4 teaspoons freshly ground
black pepper

2 tablespoons chopped fresh
rosemary, or 1 tablespoon
dried

2 tablespoons chopped fresh
thyme, or 1 tablespoon
dried

1 tablespoon kosher salt

1 large onion, diced

2 carrots, diced

2 parsnips or turnips, diced

5 cloves garlic, minced

2 tablespoons red wine
vinegar

2 tablespoons Dijon mustard

2 tablespoons tomato paste

2 cups dry white wine

2 cups chicken stock

2 bay leaves

1½ cups pitted prunes,
cut in half lengthwise

Piece of parchment
to cover shanks while
cooking

braised lamb shanks with cinnamon, prunes, and baked polenta

Because the lamb shanks and the polenta bake at different temperatures, plan on cooking the shanks ahead of time and rewarming for service. If you're lucky enough to have two ovens, cook them simultaneously.

STEP 1 Mix ¼ cup olive oil, cinnamon, pepper, rosemary, thyme, and salt in a small bowl. Spread evenly over lamb shanks and marinate for 4 to 6 hours, or overnight in the refrigerator.

STEP 2 Place an oven rack in the middle of the oven and preheat oven to 250°.

STEP 3 Preheat a large skillet (that has a tight-fitting lid) or Dutch oven over medium-high heat and add remaining 2 tablespoons of olive oil. In batches, brown shanks on all sides, making sure not to burn the spices, about 5 to 7 minutes per batch. Remove shanks and set aside.

STEP 4 Reduce heat to medium and add onion, carrot, parsnips or turnips, and sauté until soft and beginning to brown, about 7 to 10 minutes.

STEP 5 Add garlic, red wine vinegar, mustard, tomato paste, white wine, stock, and bay leaves. Over medium-high heat, bring to a full simmer, stirring the bottom of the pan to scrape up any brown bits.

STEP 6 Reduce heat to medium and return lamb shanks to the skillet or Dutch oven, making sure they are mostly submerged in liquid. Bring to a gentle simmer.

STEP 7 Wet and crumble a piece of parchment paper and place directly on top of shanks. Cover skillet or Dutch oven with lid and bake in center of oven for 3½ to 4 hours, or until fork tender.

STEP 8 Stir in prunes and cook for another 1 to 1½ hours, until meat is very tender.

STEP 9 Discard parchment paper, remove shanks to a plate, and cover them loosely with foil.

STEP 10 Over medium-high heat, reduce cooking liquid by half, to about 2 cups, and remove from heat. Taste for salt and pepper.

STEP 11 If shanks are cooked before the polenta, or the day before serving (the flavors will be better the next day), refrigerate shanks and sauce separately. Over low heat, gently reheat sauce before adding shanks.

STEP 12 If shanks and polenta are cooked at the same time, return shanks to warm sauce before serving.

POLENTA

2 cups polenta, or coarsely
ground cornmeal

10 cups water

2 tablespoons olive oil

2 teaspoons kosher salt

baked polenta

STEP 1 Preheat oven to 350°. Oil or butter a large ovenproof Dutch oven or casserole dish.

STEP 2 Add all ingredients to baking dish, stirring to make sure everything is well combined.

STEP 3 Bake uncovered in center of oven for 1 hour and 15 minutes. Stir polenta and bake for an additional 15 minutes.

STEP 4 Serve polenta in individual dishes or in an oiled serving dish.

classroom
garden
kitchen

LOPEZ ISLAND FARM EDUCATION (L.I.F.E. Garden Program)
Suzanne Berry and Valerie Yukluk

SINCE 2003, THE LOPEZ ISLAND FARM EDUCATION (L.I.F.E. Garden Program) has helped Lopez School K-12 students develop an appreciation for nature, nutrition, community, land stewardship, and the environment. Elementary students apply science and math principles in the school's Rishi Garden, orchard, and cafeteria beds; later they see the harvest of organic tomatoes, carrots, potatoes, kale, turnips, beets, and broccoli in the lunch line. "It's kind of a big puzzle," says Valerie Yukluk, "trying to figure out what the kitchen wants and what Suzanne and I know we can grow with the kids." During the growing season, the school estimates that 60-70% of vegetables served in the cafeteria are from the garden, and classes in the school kitchen teach culinary skills. For high school students, an elective class allows them to experience the entire "seed-to-plate" cycle at nearby S & S Homestead. Valerie sums up the L.I.F.E. Garden Program: "It connects kids with their food and nature. They see the living systems and how they're a part of them."

"In the garden, kids learn one of farming's important lessons— pull the weeds before they go to seed!"

MAKES 6 INDIVIDUAL FLANS

2 cloves garlic, cut in half
   lengthwise
Butter to butter ramekins
4 to 5 small summer squash,
   same or mixed varieties
2 teaspoons kosher salt
3 large eggs, beaten
¼ cup heavy cream
¼ cup whole milk
¼ cup feta or chèvre,
   crumbled
2 tablespoons grated
   Parmesan or other hard
   cheese
1 tablespoon finely chopped
   fresh mint
1 tablespoon finely chopped
   fresh marjoram or oregano
½ teaspoon kosher salt
½ teaspoon freshly ground
   black pepper

wilted summer squash flan

STEP 1 Preheat oven to 375°.

STEP 2 Rub the insides of 6 ramekins with cut sides of the garlic cloves and butter.

STEP 3 Slice the summer squash with a mandolin, or by hand, into ¼-inch slices. Put sliced squash into a colander in the sink and sprinkle with salt. Toss to evenly distribute salt and let sit for 30 minutes, occasionally tossing colander to assist with draining process.

STEP 4 Squeeze summer squash slices by hand to remove any remaining liquid, then taste for salt. If it's too salty, give squash a quick rinse and another quick squeeze.

STEP 5 Evenly distribute squash in prepared ramekins.

STEP 6 In a bowl, combine eggs, cream, milk, cheeses, herbs, and salt and pepper. Mix well and pour over squash in ramekins.

STEP 7 Using either a butter knife, or your finger, adjust custard mixture and squash to be evenly distributed in each ramekin.

STEP 8 Bake for 30 minutes or until flans are golden brown and just set.

STEP 9 Allow flan to cool for 5 minutes before inverting onto individual plates.

experimentation
improvisation
algae

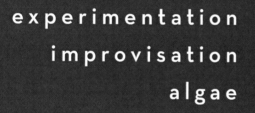

LOPEZ ISLAND SHELLFISH FARM AND HATCHERY
Sara and Nick Jones

THREE ACRES OF TIDELANDS plus a three-acre tidal lagoon on Lopez Island's Shoal Bay create an ideal environment for Lopez Island Shellfish Farm and Hatchery, another component of Jones Family Farm. The farm's shellfish—mussels; Manila, Littleneck and Butter clams; and Pacific, Flat, and Olympia oysters—benefit from being fed and sheltered in a warm, protected bay. Twice a day, clean, cold water from the Straits flushes across the beach and into the lagoon. Nick Jones credits this combination for producing "fat, sweet, robust shellfish with the fine, clean flavor usually associated with oysters grown in deep water suspension."

Buildings near the lagoon house the shellfish hatchery. Seemingly miles of PVC pipe draw water from the lagoon, circulate it through dozens of tanks that hold millions of baby oysters and clams, and return it to the lagoon. Nick's "constant experimentation and improvisation" have helped make Lopez Island Shellfish Farm and Hatchery the largest supplier of clam and oyster seed to independent shellfish farms in the region.

"With farming, there's always something new
to look forward to."

SERVES 4 AS A MAIN DISH
AND 6 AS AN APPETIZER

CLAMS

3 tablespoons olive oil

4 ounces Soppresatta
or dry salami, cut into
¼-inch matchsticks

1 large leek, cut in half
and thinly sliced

2 cloves garlic, roughly
chopped

1 3-inch hot pepper,
very thinly sliced,
or ½ teaspoon crushed red
pepper

¼ cup dry white wine

2 ripe, medium-sized
tomatoes, or 4 whole
canned tomatoes,
roughly chopped

4 pounds fresh littleneck,
Pacific littleneck, or Manila
clams, scrubbed and rinsed

2 tablespoons roughly
chopped fresh parsley

TOAST

1 loaf crusty bread, cut into
¾-inch slices, one to two
slices per person

4 or more cloves of garlic,
peeled and cut in half
lengthwise

2 ripe tomatoes, cut in half

Olive oil for drizzling

Kosher salt

clams with white wine and soppresatta

STEP 1 In a large deep skillet, or an 8-quart shallow stockpot, heat olive oil until shimmering and sauté Soppresatta for 3 minutes or until slightly crisped.

STEP 2 Add leek, garlic, and hot pepper and cook over medium heat until leek softens.

STEP 3 Over high heat, add white wine and tomatoes and bring to simmer.

STEP 4 Stir clams into simmering liquid and cover for 2 minutes. To prevent clams from overcooking, lift lid, use tongs to remove clams as they open, and transfer to a warm serving dish. Discard any clams that don't open.

STEP 5 Sprinkle chopped parsley into cooking liquid, and gently pour broth over cooked clams, making sure to leave any sand behind.

scrubbed tomato toast

STEP 1 While clams cook, toast bread slices under broiler until golden brown.

STEP 2 Remove toasted bread from broiler and immediately scrub toasts with the cut side of garlic clove, followed by the cut side of a tomato.

STEP 3 Drizzle with olive oil, sprinkle with salt, and enjoy with the clams and clam broth.

nature

nurture

ecology

LOPEZ ISLAND VINEYARDS

Brent Charnley and Maggie Nilan

BRENT CHARNLEY'S DREAMS OF A SMALL FARM and a low-impact livelihood began to coalesce in 1979 as he hitchhiked through France. He serendipitously found work on a vineyard in the Bordeaux region and learned pruning, tractor driving, and other farming skills. "I quickly found I was in love with growing grape vines!" Brent says. Eventually, he and Maggie leased land on Lopez Island, chosen because its southwest exposure and slope, plus its location in the Olympic Mountains' rainshadow, made it ideal for two early-ripening European varieties, Madeleine Angevine and Siegerrebe. As a bonus, those fields had been farmed without pesticides since they were first cleared over a hundred years earlier. It's now one of only four certified organic vineyards in Washington. In 1987 they planted three acres, using plants they'd rooted and grown themselves. "We supported the vines with posts and stakes made from cedar we'd collected from island beaches," Brent says. Since then, they've expanded the vineyard to six acres and built a winery.

"We strive for an ecosystem to produce wine that's clean and healthy and to use organic farming methods that are gentle to our bodies, our workers, and our neighbors."

SERVES 4

¼ cup minced shallot

⅓ cup Madeleine Angevine wine (may substitute dry Riesling or Gewürztraminer)

¼ cup blood orange juice

¼ cup champagne vinegar or white balsamic

½ teaspoon kosher salt

½ teaspoon sugar

½ teaspoon freshly ground black pepper

2 tablespoons very finely shredded flat-leaf parsley

24 fresh, locally-sourced oysters such as Olympia, Pacific, Kumamoto, or Shigoku

Oyster knife and clean kitchen towel for shucking

Crushed ice for serving oysters

oysters on the half shell with madeleine angevine and blood orange mignonette

STEP 1 In a bowl combine shallots, white wine, blood orange juice, vinegar, salt, sugar, and black pepper. Set aside.

STEP 2 Gently brush and rinse outside of oysters to remove any dirt.

STEP 3 Fold kitchen towel into quarters and insert an oyster, sandwiched between the folds, cup side down, with hinge just exposed.

STEP 4 Place one hand on top of the oyster to secure it while opening, keeping fingers clear of the hinge and oyster knife.

STEP 5 Gently, but assertively, insert just the tip of the oyster knife into hinge of the oyster. Twist the knife to release the hinge. Remove the knife and wipe blade clean on the kitchen towel.

STEP 6 Release the oyster from the top shell by sweeping the oyster knife between the oyster and the top shell, maintaining contact between the knife blade and inside of shell to protect the oyster.

STEP 7 While holding the lower shell that contains the oyster, carefully sweep under the oyster with the oyster knife, releasing the meat from the bottom shell while keeping oyster juice in the shell.

STEP 8 Put 1½ teaspoons of mignonette sauce on each oyster and top with a pinch of shredded parsley.

STEP 9 Place oysters in a shallow serving dish on a bed of crushed ice. Enjoy with a chilled glass of the wine used in the mignonette.

community

compost

vitality

MIDNIGHT'S FARM
David Bill and Faith Van De Putte

DAVID BILL AND FAITH VAN DE PUTTE love to eat well and share the abundance of Midnight's Farm with family, friends, visitors, and the community. They observe, "People are hungry, not just for delicious food, but for a deeper connection to the land."

Their farm is home to three families, two ponds, pigs, cattle, pasture, wetlands, gardens, an old orchard, Barn Owl Bakery, a yoga studio, and the first Department of Ecology-certified compost facility in San Juan County.

With the varied activities of the farm, "keeping it simple" and keeping it all running (from the tub grinder, to irrigation hoses, to the website) are the challenges. Yet Faith and David find joy watching cows kick up their heels when going into new pasture and seeing the steam rise from turned compost. They find hope in the face of climate change with hands-on solutions: diverting material from burn piles, sequestering carbon, and contributing to Lopez's vibrant food system. For them, farming is "the ultimate interface between humanity and nature."

"We farm to steward this wonderfully beautiful piece of the earth and for the tangible, hands-dirty love of connecting people to the soil and storing a little bit of carbon there, too."

MAKES ONE 8- OR 9-INCH
PIE

1¼ cups all-purpose flour

½ teaspoon salt

1 tablespoon sugar

6 tablespoons unsalted butter,
    cut into ¼-inch pieces, and
    chilled

4 tablespoons lard, chilled

3 to 4 tablespoons ice water

3 eggs, whites and yolks
    separated

1 cup sugar

¼ cup butter, at room
    temperature

1 teaspoon vanilla extract

¼ cup flour

¼ teaspoon salt

3 cups ½-inch pieces of
    rhubarb

rhubarb custard pie in a lard and butter crust

STEP 1 In the bowl of a food processor, mix flour, ½ teaspoon salt, and 1 tablespoon sugar. Sprinkle butter pieces on top of flour, and toss with a little flour mixture to coat . Pulse food processor for 1 second, 4 to 5 times, to cut in butter. Add lard and pulse for 1 second, 3 to 4 times, or until most of mixture resembles coarse corn meal and any remaining butter bits are no larger than small peas. Turn mixture into a medium-sized bowl. Alternatively, in a medium-sized bowl, cut butter and lard into flour mixture with two forks or a pastry cutter.

STEP 2 Sprinkle 3 tablespoons of water onto flour mixture. Using the flat side of a spatula, lift mixture from the bottom of the bowl and press down on the top of it until the pie dough sticks together. Add another tablespoon of water if dough won't come together.

STEP 3 Gather dough into a ball with your hands, press into a 4-inch disc, wrap in plastic wrap, and refrigerate for at least 30 minutes before rolling out.

STEP 4 If pie dough has been refrigerated for more than 30 minutes, let it rest on the counter for 10 minutes before rolling out. On a lightly floured surface, roll out dough into a 12-inch circle, about ⅛ inch thick.

STEP 5 Transfer dough to pie plate by rolling it up on your rolling pin and unrolling it onto pie plate. Alternatively, fold the dough circle gently into quarters, transfer to pie plate using a spatula, put the point at the center of the pie plate, and unfold. Adjust dough so that it lines the bottom and sides of pie plate.

STEP 6 Trim dough edge to hang over pie plate lip by ½ inch. Tuck the trimmed edge underneath itself so that the folded edge is about ¼ of an inch taller than the pie plate rim. Flute dough edge as desired or decorate it with the tines of a fork. Return pie shell to refrigerator while preparing filling.

STEP 7 Preheat oven to 375°.

STEP 8 In the bowl of a mixer, using the whisk attachment, beat egg whites, gradually adding ¼ cup sugar, until soft peaks form. Remove to a clean bowl.

STEP 9 Add yolks to unwashed mixing bowl, and add remaining ¾ cup sugar, butter, vanilla extract, flour, and salt. Using the paddle attachment, beat until butter is completely mixed into eggs, about 30 seconds.

STEP 10 Using a spoon, mix rhubarb pieces into yolk mixture. Add ½ of whipped egg whites, and using a clean spatula, gently fold whites into yolk mixture. When ribbons of white are still visible, add the remaining whipped egg whites and continue to fold together until just incorporated.

STEP 11 Scrape filling into chilled pie shell and bake in the lower half of oven for 30 minutes.

STEP 12 Reduce heat to 350° and bake for 30 more minutes, or until top of pie is set, and top and crust are nicely browned.

STEP 13 Cool at room temperature for one hour before slicing and serving.

patience
springtime
growth

NORFELD FARM
Danáh Feldman and Ron Norman

WHILE DANÁH FELDMAN HAS BEEN GROWING flowers and food for 35 years, farming is a new venture for her husband, Ron Norman, a mechanic and metal sculptor. Danáh delights in playing a part in what she calls "the magic of food and flowers emerging out of the soil." Ron enjoys the new challenge of plowing, planting, and harvesting a field of grain. They both revel in the tenacity of seeds and plants to poke their way through the ground. Early every spring, Danáh starts over a thousand tomato and vegetable plants—many from her own seed, and all grown organically—in her greenhouse. Dozens of repeat customers buy the starts to transplant into gardens across San Juan County. Throughout the year, Danáh also tends "a zillion flowers," vegetables, and fruit trees in the couple's 2½-acre garden.

Both Danáh and Ron love a challenge and to push the envelope; they do so in most aspects of their lives, and working with the soil is no exception. Their current garden, along with a smattering of fields on the island and a new piece of property they're developing for a farm and home, are all places to continue experimenting. "We're both inspired and compelled to go beyond what many people think is possible."

"We're doing a dance with nature,
seeing what music we can create together."

YIELDS 7 QUARTS

INGREDIENTS

1 cup lemon juice
    or 3½ teaspoons citric
    acid powder
Kosher salt
21 pounds tomatoes,
    firm, ripe, freshly picked,
    and blemish free

EQUIPMENT

7 wide mouth quart jars,
    free of chips and cracks
7 wide mouth metal screw
    bands with new metal lids
Large pot of boiling water
    for blanching tomatoes
Ice water to cool blanched
    tomatoes
Large, non-reactive pot
    for heating tomatoes
Boiling water to top off jars
Rubber or plastic spatula
7-quart capacity (or greater)
    pressure canner with
    weighted gauge

canned tomatoes (hot pack, pressure canning method)

Canning times given are for altitudes of less than 1000 ft. Because the temperature of boiling water decreases as elevation increases, if you are canning at elevations above 1000 ft., please contact your County Extension Office for accurate canning times and pressures to ensure a safe end product. Before you get started, thoroughly read pressure canner instructions and familiarize yourself with this canning method.

STEP 1 Wash canning jars and lids in hot soapy water, rinse well, and allow to dry on a clean surface. In order to maintain the integrity of the gasket on the metal lids, do not soak the lids in hot water.

STEP 2 Put 2 tablespoons lemon juice or ½ teaspoon citric acid powder into each clean quart jar. You may add 1 teaspoon salt to each jar (optional).

STEP 3 To blanch tomatoes, wash tomatoes and dip, a few at a time, into boiling water until skin splits, about 30 to 60 seconds.

STEP 4 To stop the cooking process, quickly cool tomatoes in an ice water bath, peel (discard peel), cut in half and place in a large, non-reactive pot, making sure to capture all juices.

STEP 5 Bring tomatoes and collected juice to boil over medium heat, stirring often. If the level of liquid does not cover the tomatoes by the time the pot comes to a simmer, add enough boiling water to cover the tomatoes. Gently boil for 5 minutes.

STEP 6 Quickly and carefully fill jars with hot tomato mixture leaving ¾ inch of headspace in each jar. Remove air bubbles from each jar by inserting the spatula between the food and the jar and moving the spatula up and down as you turn the jar around gently. If needed, top off the jars with more hot liquid.

STEP 7 Wipe jar rims with a clean, damp towel. Place jar lids on each jar and secure with metal band per manufacturer's instructions (not too tight, not too loose). Do not retighten metal bands after canning as it may jeopardize the seal on the processed jars.

STEP 8 Put 2 to 3 inches of hot water in the pressure canner and place filled jars in canning rack. Close canner lid and seal per manufacturer's instructions.

STEP 9 Remove weighted pressure gauge. Over high heat, bring canning pot to boil until a steady stream of steam comes from the steam vent. Keeping the heat on high, exhaust steam for 10 minutes. Place weighted gauge on vent on the 10 pound PSI mark.

STEP 10 The canner will pressurize in about 5 minutes. Once the pressure gauge reaches 10 pound PSI and the weighted gauge jiggles slightly, set a timer for 25 minutes. Adjust the heat under the canner to maintain a constant reading of 10 pound PSI, and the weighted gauge jiggles 2 or 3 times per minute. Avoid big temperature swings and dips in pressure.

STEP 11 After 25 minutes at a constant 10 pound PSI, turn off the heat and leave the canner untouched to depressurize. Do not do anything to speed up the depressurizing process; doing so may compromise the safety of your canned tomatoes.

STEP 12 Once the canner has depressurized, remove the weighted gauge, and let the canner sit for 2 to 5 minutes before carefully removing the lid.

STEP 13 Using a jar lifter, remove jars to a rack, leaving 1 to 2 inches between jars for proper cooling.

STEP 14 Check the seals on the jars after 12 to 24 hours. Push thumbs firmly into the center of each jar lid. If there is no movement in jar lid, it is sealed. If the lid springs back when you remove your finger, the jar is not sealed. Refrigerate jars that don't seal and use them within the week. Alternatively, if you are processing more tomatoes, remove the ring and lid from the unsealed jar, add more hot liquid if necessary, use a new lid, and process with the next batch.

STEP 15 Date the jars, store in a cool, dry, dark cabinet, and use within the year.

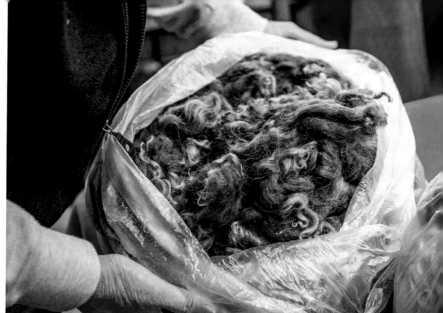

efficiency
beauty
community

ONE CLAY HILL FARM AND STONECREST JAM
Susan and David Corbin

FOR NEW MEXICO NATIVE DAVID CORBIN, Navajo–Churro sheep were what "real sheep" looked like. "Their wool colors and variations in pattern bring me back to the beauty of New Mexico where I lived as a child," David says. But this old breed, brought to the Southwest by Spanish explorers over 500 years ago, was down to only 400 animals in the 1970s. Susan and David joined with the Navajo–Churro Sheep Association in a preservation movement that has brought this previously endangered breed back from the brink of extinction.

The Heritage Navajo–Churro sheep the Corbins raise are small, independent animals known for their long, double-coat fleeces and mild, sweet meat. One Clay Hill Farm offers USDA-approved lamb as well as high luster, long wool sheepskins and raw wool for spinning. When not tending sheep, the Corbins also produce Stonecrest Jam. Hand-crafted varieties include Ginger Rhubarb, Blackberry Plum, and Apple Butter. "Since Susan and I began this endeavor in 1996, we've gained new insights and improved our activities every year," David says. "And we're certainly not through learning."

"Navajo–Churro sheep require little assistance in lambing,
they're good mothers and are rarely sick,
and they generally disdain human assistance.
Who wouldn't want to raise animals like that?"

SERVES 6

6 tablespoons unsalted butter

2 cups diced rhubarb

¼ cup brown sugar

1 teaspoon ground cinnamon

Juice of one lemon

6 eggs

1 ½ cups whole milk

1 ½ cups all-purpose flour

¼ teaspoon kosher salt

1 teaspoon vanilla extract

Stonecrest Ginger Rhubarb
  Jam

Plain, whole milk yogurt

Powdered sugar for garnish

rhubarb oven pancake with rhubarb ginger jam and yogurt

STEP 1 Preheat oven to 425°.

STEP 2 Heat a medium-sized skillet over medium-high heat. Add butter to pan, and when foaming subsides, add rhubarb. Toss rhubarb to coat with butter and cook until rhubarb is tender, but not falling apart. Remove from heat and add brown sugar, cinnamon, and lemon juice. Stir to coat.

STEP 3 Preheat a 12-inch, oven-proof skillet in the oven for 3 minutes. Using oven mitts, remove skillet from oven and distribute rhubarb in it evenly, making sure to scrape all butter and bits along with it.

STEP 4 In a mixing bowl, using a whisk or immersion blender, mix together the eggs, milk, flour, salt, and vanilla extract until smooth. Alternatively, mix ingredients in a blender.

STEP 5 Immediately pour the batter over the hot fruit and return the pan to the oven. Bake for 20 minutes, or until puffed and golden brown. Let cool for 3 minutes before serving.

STEP 6 Dollop jam and yogurt onto whole oven pancake, or on individual pieces. Dust with powdered sugar before serving.

variety
reward
beauty

RED GATE

FARM

RED GATE FARM
Marianne and Read Langenbach, Valerie and John Yukluk

READ LANGENBACH'S PERSISTENCE with his property has paid off. Although the land had long been farmed, when Read purchased it in the early 1970s from cattle farmer T. J. Blake, it was an empty cow pasture. "Every tree you see on the property, we've planted over the years," Read says. In those early days before he installed a watering system, the fruit trees (fifty of them now, mostly apple) were watered by hand.

An attorney in Seattle by day, Read describes himself as a weekend farmer who "lucked into the ideal arrangement" with John and Valerie Yukluk as neighbors. Valerie grew up on Lopez and raised sheep ("about 100 head") as a kid. Now she serves as the Red Gate Farm manager, caring for the farm's 100% grass-fed Suffolk and Texel sheep. Red Gate uses the local USDA-approved Mobile Processing Unit for their lamb, all of which they sell within San Juan County. "Raising sheep is just part of me," Valerie says. "I've been doing it most of my life."

"I feel strongly that the property is far more attractive in farm use."

SERVES 4 TO 6

1 cup all-purpose flour

1 cup whole wheat pastry flour
   or all-purpose flour

¼ teaspoon salt

2 tablespoons baking powder

8 tablespoons unsalted
   butter, room temperature,
   cut into ¼-inch pieces

6 to 8 tablespoons whole milk

4 to 6 (about 2 pounds)
   baking apples

1 juicy lemon

Milk to seal and brush the
   dumplings

1 cup heavy cream or ice
   cream for serving

FOR EACH APPLE:

1 tablespoon unsalted butter,
   room temperature

1 tablespoon sugar

1 teaspoon cinnamon

apple dumplings

STEP 1 Preheat oven to 400°. Line a half-sheet pan with parchment paper.

STEP 2 In a bowl, mix together flours, salt, baking powder, and butter. Cut butter into dry ingredients until the mixture resembles coarse corn meal. Alternatively, pulse ingredients together in a food processor.

STEP 3 Sprinkle 6 tablespoons of milk over the dry mixture and mix with a fork to combine. If dough is too dry, add more milk, one tablespoon at a time, until the dough just comes together.

STEP 4 Using your hands, gently knead dough until it forms a ball.

STEP 5 Peel and core apples and sprinkle liberally with lemon juice.

STEP 6 On a lightly floured surface, roll out dough into a large square, ¼-inch thick. Cut into individual squares big enough to cover each apple.

STEP 7 Place an apple in the middle of each dough square. Into each core, add 1 teaspoon cinnamon, 1 tablespoon sugar, and 1 tablespoon butter.

STEP 8 Brush all 4 edges of the dough square with milk. Bring two adjacent corners together at a time, pinching the edges to seal them, creating four wings. Bring the sealed corners towards the center and pinch at the top of the apple to secure. Brush all sides of the apple with milk and fold the four wings, in the same clockwise direction, sealing them to the sides of the apple.

STEP 9 Place apples on prepared baking sheet and bake for 40 to 45 minutes, or until dumplings are a deep, golden brown and steaming.

STEP 10 Allow dumplings to cool for 15 minutes before serving. At the table, break individual dumplings open and drizzle generously with heavy cream or ice cream.

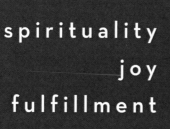

spirituality

joy

fulfillment

S & S HOMESTEAD FARM
Elizabeth Simpson and Henning Sehmsdorf

ELIZABETH SIMPSON AND HENNING SEHMSDORF'S goal for their 50-acre, biodynamic farm is to feed themselves, their animals, and their soil from farm-grown resources. They also strive to produce wood products from their small forest as well as their own electricity and water. The farm shares its yield through a whole-diet CSA (Community Supported Agriculture) program and sales at the Lopez Farmers Market.

Both Henning and Elizabeth are veteran teachers, and they put those skills to work at the farm's S & S Center for Sustainable Agriculture. An elective class for Lopez High School students introduces them to the entire "seed-to-plate" cycle at the farm. The students prepare soil, plant crops, and care for the farm's cows, sheep, pigs and chickens. The Center also involves apprentices and interns in all aspects of the whole farm organism. Their workshops, farm tours, and classes cover a wide variety of topics, including farm economics; machine maintenance; vegetable production and seed saving; animal husbandry; pasture management; grain production; and bread-baking, fermentation, and cheese- and butter-making. "Our hope through these efforts," they say, "is that our farm and programs will continue beyond our working lifetime."

"One of the most important lessons we've learned as farmers is to listen to the land, the plants, and the animals."

MAKES 10 TO 12
(2½-INCH) CAKES,
SERVES 4

GRIDDLE CAKES

1 cup dried, whole-kernel,
    flint (or Indian) corn

1 teaspoon baking soda

3 strips of good quality bacon,
    uncooked, and cut into
    ½-inch strips

2 eggs

2 teaspoons olive oil

½ cup finely minced onion

2 cloves garlic, finely minced

2 tablespoons finely minced
    fresh herbs: parsley,
    thyme, sage, chives,
    or any combination

Kosher salt and freshly ground
    black pepper to taste

4 to 5 teaspoons all-purpose
    flour

Unsalted butter and olive oil
    for cooking

GREENS

1 bunch of collard greens,
    1½ to 2 pounds, washed

¼ pound good quality bacon,
    cut into ½-inch pieces

1 to 2 tablespoons apple cider
    vinegar

1 to 2 tablespoons water

Freshly ground black pepper

corn griddle cakes with collard greens and bacon

STEP 1 Cover corn kernels with 2 inches of water and soak in the refrigerator for two days.

STEP 2 Simmer corn and baking soda in soaking liquid for several hours, over medium-low heat, until tender. Add more water as needed to keep corn submerged while cooking. Remove from heat and cool to room temperature.

STEP 3 Heat 2 teaspoons olive oil in a small skillet over medium-high heat. Cook onion until translucent and just beginning to brown. Remove from heat.

STEP 4 In the bowl of a food processor, purée cooked corn, bacon, eggs, onion, garlic, herbs, and spices. While pulsing, add enough flour to form a soft and pliable dough. Add salt and pepper to taste, keeping in mind that the bacon will add salt as the cakes cook.

STEP 5 In a skillet preheated over medium-high heat, melt 1 tablespoon butter with 1 tablespoon olive oil. When butter foams, add heaping spoonsful of dough to the skillet, leaving enough room to flatten and turn the cakes.

STEP 6 Flatten cakes and flip when the underside is nicely browned. Cook the second side until it is nicely browned as well.

STEP 7 Add more butter and olive oil to the skillet as needed between batches to prevent sticking.

STEP 8 Cakes hold well in a warm oven until they are ready to be served on top of, or alongside of, the Collard Greens and Bacon.

collard greens and bacon

STEP 1 Stack collard leaves and cut them into 1-inch ribbons.

STEP 2 Cook bacon in a skillet large enough for the greens, over medium-high heat, until fat renders and the bacon is lightly crisped. Use a slotted spoon to remove the bacon to a bowl.

STEP 3 Add greens to the bacon fat left in the skillet and cook over medium-high heat, stirring often, until slightly wilted.

STEP 4 Reduce heat to low and pour vinegar and water evenly over greens, stirring to coat evenly.

STEP 5 Cover the skillet and cook greens for 3 to 5 minutes, stirring occasionally, until the greens have wilted but retain their bright green color.

STEP 6 Return the bacon to the skillet with the greens, toss to combine, and add pepper and salt to taste.

scent
touch
taste

SKYRIVER RANCH
Irene Skyriver

FROM THE TIME OF HER FIRST GARDEN over forty years ago, stories from Irene Skyriver's grandparents and parents have motivated her. They weathered the Great Depression working hard, but eating well, on a farm in Monroe, Washington. "My grandfather's spirit whispers to take up the hoe," she says.

Now, as Irene stewards Lopez land purchased in 1968, she views growing food as a sacred obligation that also "feeds" her in many ways. Pruning, weeding, shoveling, milking goats, and harvesting serve as her yoga class, meditation, aerobics, medicine chest, teacher, and sanctuary. Irene feels "blessed by all of this, plus year-round organic food in my larders and enough income from plant starts and produce sales at the Southend General Store to cover each year's start-up costs." Irene explains that she's not "scientific" in her gardening approach of saving seeds and letting plants volunteer. "I make no claims in favor of my methods," she says, "but they work for me!"

"As the swallows miraculously arrive each spring,
so have I learned to trust my instincts in my garden dance.
I'm drawn like a compass needle into my garden
and greenhouse, pulled, as the moon pulls the tides,
to seed those first tomatoes, peppers, and peas."

**MAKES ABOUT 6 CUPS
COOKED BEANS**

2 cups best quality dried beans

2 to 4 cloves of garlic

1 bay leaf

1 sprig of thyme, sage,
   or both

6 whole black peppercorns

2 tablespoons olive oil

Salt to taste

frances kring beans with herbs, garlic, and olive oil

Frances Kring beans have been grown on Lopez Island for at least 75 years (Frances was born here in 1917). Closely related to scarlet runner beans, the Frances Krings resemble lima beans in appearance and are creamy, rich and earthy. Any dried beans will work in this recipe, and with the current availability of local and heirloom beans, it is well worth the effort to source such varieties to experience their large range of flavor, texture, and color.

STEP 1 To soak beans overnight, pour beans through your fingers (looking for any small rocks or debris) into a bowl. Cover with several inches of water and refrigerate overnight. To quick-soak your beans, cover beans with several inches of water in a large heavy-bottomed pot and bring to a boil. Remove beans from the heat, cover, and let sit for an hour.

STEP 2 If beans were soaked overnight, put beans and soaking liquid into a heavy-bottomed pot. If beans were quick-soaked, return pot to stovetop. Top off beans with a few more inches of water and return to stovetop (no need to pour off soaking liquid).

STEP 3 Smash peeled garlic cloves with the side of a chef's knife and add to bean pot with herbs, peppercorns, and olive oil.

STEP 4 Gently simmer beans, partially covered, until beans are tender. Add water, if needed, to keep beans submerged while cooking. Once beans are tender, add salt until the cooking liquid is the desired saltiness. If added too early in the cooking process, salt will toughen the bean skins. The same rule applies for adding any acidic ingredients to your beans, like tomatoes. Wait until the beans are mostly cooked before adding. As beans continue to cook, they'll absorb the salt.

STEP 5 Once beans are cooked, remove from heat and let cool in their cooking liquid.

STEP 6 The beans are now ready to use in other recipes or to serve and eat. Make sure to save and use the delicious bean cooking broth; it's too good to waste.

STEP 7 Drizzle beans and broth with a little olive oil, and serve in shallow bowls. Enjoy with crusty bread.

breathing
goats
home

SUNNYFIELD FARM
Elizabeth and Andre Entermann

FOR YEARS, ANDRE ENTERMANN didn't want to be a farmer; he thought of farming as contributing to the destruction of the planet. An apprenticeship at Horse Drawn Farm, and actually getting to know a family farm committed to environmentally conscious farming, changed his views. It also inspired Andre to follow his dream to start a goat dairy. Along the way, he met Elizabeth and found that she shared his appreciation for goats. "They have the potential to be low-impact," Andre says, "by making milk off of wild, native forage." The couple attended workshops and visited countless farms, then made modifications at Sunnyfield Farm. In the 1930s, the farm (now owned by Elizabeth's dad, Ron Metcalf) was a cow dairy, complete with barn, milking stalls, and outbuildings for processing milk and cheese. Today, a herd of Alpine goats feels right at home there, and Sunnyfield has a Washington State Department of Agriculture Grade A license to produce and sell raw goat milk, aged cheese, and chèvre. "Becoming a licensed dairy seemed like the impossible," Andre says, yet it taught him some of farming's most important lessons: "Be patient, learn from others, and don't be afraid to wing it."

"Being part of the local food producers' stream totally aligns with my values. Plus, I get to live and work at home, take a break and go to the house to see my family and have a cup of coffee, then go back to the goats."

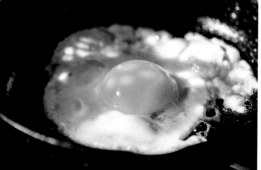

MAKES 2 SANDWICHES

3 tablespoons unsalted butter

4 (¾-inch thick) slices of
rustic bread

4 ounces chèvre

1 large, ripe tomato,
cut into ½-inch slices

2 large eggs

1 tablespoon olive oil

1 dozen large leaves of arugula

Kosher salt and freshly ground
pepper to taste

Optional hot sauce
such as Chicaoji

hot egg sandwich with chèvre, tomato, and arugula

STEP 1 Melt 1 tablespoon of butter in a large skillet over medium-high heat. When the butter foams, place two slices of bread in the skillet and cook until golden brown. Flip slices of bread and repeat. When the second side is toasted, remove slices to a warm plate.

STEP 2 Add another tablespoon of butter to the skillet and repeat with remaining slices of bread.

STEP 3 After the second side is toasted, flip the bread to expose the first, hot, toasted side and slather with half of the chèvre. Top with 1 or 2 slices of tomato, season with salt and pepper, turn off the heat and leave the bread in the pan to stay warm while you cook the eggs.

STEP 4 Preheat a second skillet over medium-high heat and add 1 tablespoon of butter. When the butter foams, add olive oil. Carefully crack eggs into the skillet, one at a time, and season with salt and pepper. Cook for two minutes or until whites set and crisp slightly. Using a thin metal spatula, carefully flip the eggs and cook for one more minute.

STEP 5 Place the chèvre and tomato toasts on plates and top each with a cooked egg. Douse with optional hot sauce, and top each half with half of the arugula. Finish with the remaining pieces of toasted bread and enjoy with plenty of napkins—these sandwiches are delicious, but messy!

land
restoration
opportunity

SWEET GRASS FARM
Scott Meyers and Brigit Waring

SCOTT MEYERS HADN'T PLANNED TO RAISE cattle when he and his wife Brigit and their two daughters moved to a farm on Lopez in 1999. Now he says, "I'm home. I've learned how to slow down and to observe and draw my conclusions slowly, and then to be willing to revisit them and never hold them as truths." Scott grew up in a family of crop farmers and orchardists; as he considered how to restore the soil on his Lopez farmland, he recognized that cattle are a powerful tool. "They can create fertility on an unbelievable scale," he says. After much research, Scott chose to raise purebred Wagyu "Kobe" beef, a Japanese cattle breed valued for its taste, tenderness, marbling, and healthful fat content. Scott's cattle are fed a diet that is 100% grass and hay from Sweet Grass Farm pastures. Although Scott now has a healthy herd on restored farmland, he continues to learn and to savor the "newness and freshness of opportunity" that farming offers.

"Farming for me is about restoration,
improving the health and balance of the environment
I get to touch. I feel blessed to participate
with the land."

SERVES 2 TO 3

STEAK

One 16- to 24-ounce well-
  marbled steak from grass-
  fed beef (New York Strip,
  Rib Eye, Porterhouse),
  at least 1½ inches thick,
  preferably bone in.

2 to 3 teaspoons kosher salt
  (depending on size of steak)

1 teaspoon freshly ground
  black pepper

½ teaspoon freshly ground
  white pepper

¼ cup avocado oil or organic
  vegetable oil

4 tablespoons unsalted butter

pan-fried steak with anchovy gremolata

STEP 1 One day before cooking and serving steak, combine salt and ground peppers in a small bowl.

STEP 2 Dry both sides of steak and liberally coat all sides with salt and pepper mixture. Put steak on a rimmed plate, or shallow pie plate, and refrigerate, uncovered, for at least 24 hours. As juices collect in the bottom of the dish and form a concentrated brine, flip steak once or twice to evenly distribute seasoning.

STEP 3 Remove steak from refrigerator and once again dry it off thoroughly.

STEP 4 Preheat oil in a 12-inch, heavy-bottomed, cast iron skillet over high heat.

STEP 5 When oil begins to smoke, using a pair of tongs, carefully lower steak into the oil in the middle of the pan.

STEP 6 Cook steak for about 5 minutes, flipping frequently, to develop a golden brown crust.

STEP 7 Add butter to pan and baste steak with melted butter to promote even browning. If butter starts to burn, reduce heat to medium. Continue to baste and flip steak until an instant-read thermometer inserted into thickest part of steak reads 125°, about 8 minutes. This will give you a medium-rare steak. Add 5 more degrees if you'd like it cooked a bit more.

STEP 8 Remove steak from pan and allow it to rest for 5 to 10 minutes before slicing and serving with Anchovy Gremolata.

MAKES 1 CUP

GREMOLATA

1½ cups flat-leaf parsley leaves

3 to 4 garlic cloves

1 tablespoon lemon zest

2 to 3 olive oil-packed
  anchovy fillets

¼ cup freshly squeezed lemon
  juice

3 tablespoons olive oil

anchovy gremolata

STEP 1 Rough chop all dry ingredients by hand and combine with wet ingredients in a small bowl.

STEP 2 Alternatively, pulse all ingredients together in a food processor to form a coarse, chunky, paste.

community
joy
soil

SWEETBRIAR FARM
Tamara Buchanan and Doug Benoliel

With more than 70 years of experience commercially growing plants, Tamara Buchanan and Doug Benoliel started their 20-acre "new farm" in 2010. They've built it around "old ideas"—growing real food in an organic, sustainable way that supports the earth and the community. While their produce can be purchased at their Farm Stand on Center Road and is available at local eateries, they donate a significant portion to community efforts, such as The Hamlet and the Lopez Family Resource Center's "Lopez Fresh" program. Doug and Tamara are committed to sharing the work, the learning, and the joy of the Sweetbriar Farm with a team of volunteers and interns. In their experience, "Happy farmers grow Happy Food!"

*"Farming has strengthened our commitment to listen . . .
to the plants and nature, to each other,
and to our volunteers and interns."*

SERVES 6 AS A SALAD
AND 4 AS A MAIN COURSE

GRILLED CHICORIES

1 medium head radicchio,
   about 8 ounces

1 medium head escarole,
   about 8 ounces

3 heads Belgian endive

Olive oil for grilling chicories

Kosher salt for seasoning
   grilled chicories

1 pound cooked Dungeness
   crab meat

MAKES 1½ CUPS

SALSA VERDE

¾ cup lovage leaves, or celery
   leaves

½ cup sorrel leaves, or parsley

¾ cup flat-leaf parsley leaves
   (if substituting parsley for
   sorrel leaves, use a total of
   1¼ cups parsley leaves)

2 cloves garlic

1 tablespoon freshly squeezed
   lemon juice (if substituting
   parsley for sorrel leaves,
   increase to 2 tablespoons
   lemon juice and 1 teaspoon
   lemon zest)

⅔ cup extra virgin olive oil

½ teaspoon kosher salt

½ teaspoon freshly ground
   black pepper

grilled chicories with dungeness crab and sorrel-lovage salsa verde

Chicories, hearty members of the lettuce family, are pleasantly bitter when eaten raw. Cooking mellows the bitterness and brings out nuttier flavors. Both sorrel and lovage are hearty, perennial herbs that are sadly underutilized in today's kitchens. Sorrel is delightfully tart, and lovage tastes of strong celery. I've given substitutions if you can't source them.

STEP 1 Preheat a gas or charcoal grill to medium-high.

STEP 2 If the cut edges of the chicory stems are brown or discolored, trim them.

STEP 3 Cut the radicchio and escarole heads into quarters, making sure to keep the cores intact and all leaves attached to the core. Cut the Belgian endive heads in half.

STEP 4 When grill is hot, brush chicories with olive oil and grill on all sides until leaves are lightly charred and wilted, about 5 to 6 minutes. Remove from grill and sprinkle with a pinch (¼ teaspoon) or two of kosher salt.

STEP 5 When chicories are cool enough to handle, use your hands to tear the quarters into rough pieces.

STEP 6 In a serving bowl, toss grilled chicories and crab meat with enough Salsa Verde to coat everything evenly, adding more if desired.

salsa verde

STEP 1 Combine all ingredients in the bowl of a food processor and pulse to make a coarse, chunky sauce. Taste for salt and pepper and adjust as needed.

STEP 2 Extra salsa verde can be stored in the refrigerator for up to one week.

plants
animals
love

T&D FARMS

1844

T & D FARMS
Todd Goldsmith and Diane Dear

"IT'LL BE GREAT—WE'LL ALWAYS HAVE A PROJECT!" That's what Diane Dear and Todd Goldsmith thought when they bought a 40-acre parcel that was once part of the 300-acre Ellis Ranch. Since then, they've had plenty of projects. At the time of their purchase, a well was the only improvement on the parcel that was in a San Juan Preservation Trust easement to preserve farmland and wetlands. With the help of Lopez architects Nancy and Joe Greene, Todd and Diane developed a plan for a working farm to sustainably raise eggs, vegetables, fruit, hay, and plant starts. They began with 2 irrigation ponds, utility trenches, power and water lines, and limited clearing of forest. They also plowed and developed a 2-acre fenced area for row crops, raised beds, and a small fruit orchard. The first building to go up was a tractor shed, then a chicken coop and barn, and finally, the house. Diane and Todd have learned, as they say, "to enjoy the chaos," knowing that the list of things that need to be done in a day may change in a second depending on the weather, pest damage, animal needs, or equipment repairs. "We can't imagine any more fulfilling way to spend our time."

"Farming is equal parts science and magic that allows us to express our love of nature, good food, community, and hard work."

SERVES 4

1½ cups whole-grain emmer farro, or whole wheat berries

6 cups chicken or vegetable stock, preferably homemade

½ to 1 teaspoon kosher salt, depending on saltiness of stock

One 2- to 2½-pound dry-fleshed winter squash such as Blue Hubbard, Sibley, Kabocha, or Red Kuri

One 1- to 1½-pound sweet-fleshed winter squash such as Acorn, Butternut, or Delicata

Olive oil for brushing squash and for cooking vegetables

Kosher salt

1 tablespoon unsalted butter

1½ cups thinly sliced mushrooms (cremini or button)

2 cups roughly chopped savoy or green cabbage

1 tablespoon finely chopped parsley

1 teaspoon finely chopped thyme

½ teaspoon kosher salt

½ teaspoon freshly ground black pepper

4 green onions, thinly sliced on the diagonal

1 tablespoon apple cider molasses (recipe on page 12)

roasted winter squash with emmer farro, mushrooms, and apple cider molasses

Emmer, known as farro in Italy, is an ancient ancestor of wheat. It is delicious, easy to prepare, and very nutritious.

STEP 1 Preheat oven to 400°.

STEP 2 Carefully cut both squashes in half, either end to end or horizontally. The dry-fleshed squash will be stuffed, so think about how it will sit on a plate before cutting it. Remove seeds and clean out cavities.

STEP 3 Brush the cut edges and cavities of squash with olive oil and sprinkle with salt. Invert onto a rimmed baking sheet so cut sides are in contact with the baking sheet, and bake until squash are tender but not mushy, about 45 minutes to an hour. If the smaller squash cooks faster than the larger squash, remove it from the oven and set aside. Cool squash cut side up on the baking sheet.

STEP 4 Combine emmer farro, stock, and salt in a medium saucepan, and bring to simmer over medium-high heat. Reduce heat to low to maintain a slow simmer, partially cover, and cook until grains are soft but still chewy, about 50 to 60 minutes. If cooking liquid level falls below the emmer farro grains during cooking, add more stock or water to cover. Remove from heat and set aside.

STEP 5 Preheat a medium skillet over medium-high heat. Add butter and 1 tablespoon olive oil. Cook mushrooms until soft and lightly browned, about 3 minutes. Add cabbage and continue to cook until wilted, about 4 minutes.

STEP 6 Add parsley, thyme, salt, pepper, and emmer farro to skillet and toss to combine. Turn off the burner under the skillet.

STEP 7 Preheat broiler in oven and adjust oven rack to accommodate squash halves without burning.

STEP 8 Using a soup spoon or a melon baller, scoop chunks from one half of the sweet-fleshed squash and add to skillet with other vegetables. Save the other half of the squash for another use. Add green onions and mix gently to combine. Taste for salt and pepper and adjust as desired. Keep warm over low heat.

STEP 9 Once broiler is hot, place two larger squash halves, cut side up, under the broiler to brown and reheat before stuffing, about 1 minute. Make sure they don't burn. If the cut edges dried out while baking, brush with more olive oil before placing under the broiler.

STEP 10 Stuff each half of the larger squash with vegetable mixture and drizzle with olive oil and apple cider molasses before serving.

enjoyment
purpose
laughter

THE LUCKY EWE FARM
Audrey Swanberg and Michelle McDarmont

ALTHOUGH AUDREY SWANBERG GREW UP around her aunt's horse ranch and knew that farming was something she wanted to do someday, she and Michelle McDarmont consider themselves the "newbies on the block" when it comes to their lamb operation. In 2013, the couple had the opportunity to take over sheep from Oakley Goodner and Ben Kercsmar. It's quite a mix of breeds they're learning about, with North Country Coopworth, Romney, a Katahdin cross, and Icelandics. As residents of the Lopez Community Land Trust Common Ground community, Michelle and Audrey pasture their sheep at Hill Farm on Center Road. Their first year tested them mightily when they lost about a third of their lambs to the parasitic disease, toxoplasmosis. Although not an uncommon infection, its impact on their flock was gut-wrenching for the two women. Since then, lambing has gone well, and their healthy sheep have taught them, "There are good days and bad days in farming, but it all works out and is so rewarding in the end."

*"We're proud that our sheep are happy and healthy.
We've heard numerous comments about the high quality
of our meat and wool—that just doesn't happen
with unhappy sheep."*

MAKES 24 (1½-INCH)
MEATBALLS (SERVES
4 TO 6)

MEATBALLS

4 ounces crusty bread, cut
    into 2-inch cubes (about
    2 cups)

½ large onion, diced

¼ cup chopped cilantro,
    leaves and stems

¼ cup chopped mint, leaves
    and stems

1 cup chopped parsley, leaves
    and stems

4 cloves garlic

½ teaspoon kosher salt

2 teaspoons Aleppo pepper
    or ½ teaspoon red pepper
    flakes

Olive oil

2 pounds ground lamb

YOGURT SAUCE

1 cup plain yogurt

2 tablespoons olive oil

2 tablespoons lemon juice

¼ cup crumbled feta

¼ cup chopped parsley,
    leaves only

¼ cup chopped cilantro,
    leaves only

¼ cup chopped mint, leaves
    only

¼ teaspoon kosher salt

Freshly ground course black
    pepper

lamb meatballs with yogurt feta sauce

STEP 1 Soak bread in enough water to cover it and let it soak until it begins to fall apart. Squeeze out all excess water.

STEP 2 In the bowl of a food processor, pulse bread, onion, herbs, garlic, salt, and Aleppo pepper until it forms a course paste. In a large bowl, combine the paste with ground lamb and mix with your hands until well combined.

STEP 3 Fry a small patty of meatball mixture to taste and adjust seasonings as needed.

STEP 4 Cover meatball mixture and refrigerate for at least one hour.

STEP 5 While mixture chills, make yogurt sauce. Mix yogurt, olive oil, and lemon juice until well combined. Stir in feta, herbs, salt, and pepper. Set aside.

STEP 6 Form lamb mixture into 1¾-inch balls. Heat 1 to 2 tablespoons of olive oil in a heavy-bottomed, large skillet over medium-high heat. In two batches, cook meatballs until browned on all sides and cooked through, about 5 to 8 minutes.

STEP 7 Spread yogurt sauce on the bottom of a large, shallow serving dish. Place meatballs on top of sauce and garnish with a sprinkle of herbs.

community
food
flavor

WINDY BOTTOM FARM
Kim Bast and Todd Kegerreis

A LOVE OF GOOD FOOD TO FEED themselves and others is what motivates Kim Bast and Todd Kegerreis to "embrace the chaos" of creating Windy Bottom Farm. As with many Lopez Island farmers, Todd and Kim's efforts focus on developing and restoring the farm's infrastructure of water, fencing, and buildings, as well as dealing with the clay soil that turns to mud in the winter. They take pride in the care they give to the animals they raise: heritage breed pigs that are a Berkshire/Mangalitsa cross; dairy and meat goats (Nubian, Alpine, and Kiko); and a "motley, assorted crew of laying hens." Much care goes into the dozen or so varieties of garlic they raise, too, including Nootka Rose (from Waldron Island), Broad Leaf Czech, Duganski, and Brown Vesper. An unexpected joy has been trying out seeds they find in their travels or that friends give them: "We plant them and see what happens!" What happens around the Windy Bottom Farm table, though, is always delicious.

"Learning to embrace chaos has been a powerful lesson for us, and it continues to push us."

SERVES 6

1¼ cups whole milk ricotta cheese

Cheesecloth for draining ricotta

1½ pounds freshly picked stinging nettles, tender tops and leaves only, or fresh spinach or chard

3 large egg yolks, lightly beaten

1 cup freshly grated Parmigiano-Reggiano or Romano cheese

¼ teaspoon freshly grated nutmeg

½ teaspoon kosher salt

½ teaspoon freshly ground black pepper

3 to 6 tablespoons all-purpose flour, more for dusting

2 to 4 cloves of garlic

1 to 1½ cups extra virgin olive oil, more for toasting hazelnuts

1 cup raw hazelnuts

nettle gnudi with nettle garlic pesto and toasted hazelnuts

Stinging Nettles are harbingers of spring and host four butterflies native to the Salish Sea. Nettles are loaded with vitamins and minerals, and delicious when handled with care and properly cooked. To avoid the sting, wear thick gloves when harvesting the tender tops and leaves of the nettle plant. Continue to handle the nettles with care until after the preliminary blanching process as heat takes away the sting. Gnudi (pronounced "nudie") are ricotta dumplings that resemble the filling inside a ravioli (nude ravioli).

STEP 1 Drain ricotta cheese in a colander lined with cheesecloth.

STEP 2 Bring an 8-quart pot of lightly salted water to boil over high heat. Plunge nettles into boiling water and simmer for 2 minutes. Drain immediately, and when nettles are cool enough to touch (they are now sting-free), squeeze out any remaining water and roughly chop. ⅔ of the nettles are for the gnudi. Set aside ⅓ of the nettles for the pesto.

STEP 3 Finely chop the nettles for the gnudi. In a large bowl, combine the drained ricotta, finely chopped nettles, egg yolks, grated Parmesan, nutmeg, salt and pepper, and 3 tablespoons of flour. Mix well, cover, and refrigerate for at least 30 minutes.

STEP 4 In the bowl of a food processor or immersion blender, purée garlic, remaining nettles, and enough olive oil to make a loose pesto. Add salt and pepper to taste and set aside.

STEP 5 Preheat oven to 350°. Toss hazelnuts with a few teaspoons of olive oil to coat, and roast for 15 to 20 minutes, until hazelnuts toast to a dark brown. Once the nuts cool, chop them roughly with a chef's knife.

STEP 6 Bring an 8-quart pot of slightly salted water to a boil. Using a teaspoon, scoop enough chilled gnudi mixture to make a 1-inch round gnudi. Using a second teaspoon, remove the gnudi from the first spoon, and drop it gently onto a well-floured surface. Dust the gnudi with flour, and repeat with the remainder of the gnudi mixture. If the gnudi do not hold their shape, mix in more flour, 1 to 2 tablespoons at a time.

STEP 7 Once the water boils, reduce the heat to a gentle simmer. Using a slotted spoon, gently lower 1 or 2 gnudi into the water and cook gently for 3 to 4 minutes, or until they float to the surface. Remove with a slotted spoon to a lightly oiled dish. If the gnudi fall apart while cooking or you would like a firmer texture, add 2 more tablespoons of flour to the mixture. Cook remaining gnudi in 2 batches, making sure to not overcrowd the pot.

STEP 8 To serve, spoon half of the pesto into the bottom of a warmed shallow serving dish. Place gnudi on top of the pesto and drizzle with remaining pesto. Sprinkle with toasted, chopped hazelnuts and serve with grated Parmesan cheese.

The BOUNTY Team

- Kim Bast
- Sandy Bishop
- Iris Graville
- Rachel Graville
- Heather Woodruff Harrison
- Robert S. Harrison
- Steve Horn
- Jane Jeszeck
- Pamela McCabe
- Rhea Miller
- Kim Pasciuto
- Marney Reynolds
- Sue Roundy
- Summer Moon Scriver

BOUNTY
Lopez Island Farmers, Food, and Community

Published by Lopez Community Land Trust
PO Box 25
Lopez Island, Washington 98261 USA
http://www.lopezclt.org

All rights reserved.
No part of this book may be reproduced in any form, except for brief reviews, without written permission of the publisher.

Copyright ©2016
Photographs: Robert S. Harrison, Steve Horn, Summer Moon Scriver
Text: Iris Graville
Recipes: Kim Bast
Design: Jane Jeszeck/Jigsaw

ISBN 978-0-692-77598-1
Library of Congress Control Number: 2016953546
Second Edition 2016

Printed in USA by Bookmobile
5120 Cedar Lake Road
Minneapolis MN 55416

www.lopezbounty.org

Chef **Kim Bast** was fortunate to grow up under the loving tutelage of many exceptional cooks and knew at an early age that her life's focus would be food. She's prepared meals at the bottom of the Grand Canyon, base camp on Mount Rainier, and many fine kitchens in between. Kim lives with her husband and a bevy of animals at Windy Bottom Farm, where she's discovered that growing food is as much fun as cooking it.

Sandy Bishop, Executive Director of Lopez Community Land Trust (LCLT), is deeply interested in the relationship between healthy soils, healthy foods, and the overall health of our island ecosystem, with community at the center.

Writer **Iris Graville** believes everyone has a story to tell. She collaborated with BOUNTY photographer, Summer Moon Scriver, on the award-winning book *Hands at Work*—a collection of stories and photographs of people (including several BOUNTY farmers) who are passionate about work with their hands. Iris's personal essays and profiles have been published widely, and she posts regularly at irisgraville.com.

Food Stylist **Rachel Graville** has worked in the food industry for over a decade. As an entrepreneur, she founded and operated Iris Café in Brooklyn, New York, a critically acclaimed restaurant and gourmet shop. Prior to that, she was the event planner for *Edible Brooklyn* and *Edible Manhattan* magazines. Most recently, Rachel assisted Belcampo Meat Co. CEO Anya Fernald in development of her cookbook, *Home Cooked*.

Heather Woodruff Harrison works at the Lopez Island Family Resource Center. She attended Bard College as an undergraduate and obtained her Master's in Social Work from Smith College in 2012. Heather moved to Lopez a year later to live with photographer Robert S. Harrison. She enjoys serving on the board of the Lopez Locavores, a nonprofit dedicated to promoting a local, sustainable, food economy and land stewardship.

Photographer **Robert S. Harrison** is a fine art, wedding, and commercial photographer (rsharrison.com). He grew up on Lopez, and photography has been his passion since the eighth grade. It has taken him to Bard College, around the world, and ultimately back to Lopez. Since his return in 2010, Robert developed great appreciation for local farmers and lived at Sunnyfield Farm for several years, where he and his wife Heather still attend weekly dinners.

Photographer **Steve Horn** specializes in portrait, landscape and documentary work, ranging from the Balkans to Seattle's Bumbershoot Festival (stevehorn.net). Steve is a longtime Lopez resident who believes that farming is part of the island's identity and soul.

Book Designer **Jane Jeszeck** operates Jigsaw, a design studio in Seattle focusing on book and publication design (www.jigsawseattle.com). Why Jigsaw? Jane believes that the world is a puzzle with an infinite number of pieces, all of which fit if you can figure out how.

Pamela McCabe is a former nurse, counselor, mediator, and long-time community volunteer with non-profits. Work with the BOUNTY project brings together her appreciation of Lopez Island's vibrant agricultural community and her joy of growing and cooking fresh food.

Rhea Miller, Assistant to the Director of Lopez Community Land Trust (LCLT), directs the sustainable agriculture program of the LCLT, coordinates production of the Farm Products Guide, and administers the intern program. She also directed the Lopez School's L.I.F.E. Garden Program for its first year of inception.

Kim Pasciuto has a background in law and small business management. She found her true home in the Northwest in 1985 when she and husband Ciro moved from Italy to Seattle and then to Lopez in 2011. Together they founded La Panzanella, an artisan bakery in Seattle honored with the Mayor's Small Business Award in 2001. Kim's most recent focus is on sustainable food systems and agricultural policy, including Farm-to-School programs and Food Policy Councils.

Marney Reynolds brings to the BOUNTY project her graphic design skills, her love of growing food and sharing it locally, and her many years of community involvement. She serves as Co-Director of GMO–Free San Juans and is a member of the Lopez Locavores Board of Directors.

Project Manager **Sue Roundy** was trained in design and for 30 years has worked with others for the good of her communities. Growing up in Bellingham, Washington, Sue's family fished, foraged, and preserved the bounty of Whatcom County. Living on Lopez has brought her back to her Northwest locavore roots. She served on the Lopez Community Land Trust board 2008–2011 and is currently on the board of the Lopez Locavores.

Photographer **Summer Moon Scriver** has documented important events on Lopez Island— from weddings to coming-of-age ceremonies to sports events—for over twenty years. Her work has been shown in galleries throughout the Northwest as well as in the book, *Hands at Work* (handsworking.com), a collaboration with BOUNTY writer Iris Graville. Summer grew up on Lopez Island and is now raising her own family here, along with a bounty of organic foods in her various gardens.

Farm photography credits ©2014: Robert S. Harrison, pages 30, 34, 62, 82, 86, 98, 102, 106, 114. Steve Horn, pages 1, 8, 10, 14, 22, 26, 38, 46, 50 (portrait only), 58, 66, 74, 110. Summer Moon Scriver, pages 18, 42, 50, 54, 70, 78, 90, 94, 118. Heather Woodruff Harrison ©2016, page 98 (Sunnyfield Farm family portrait). Food photography by Robert S. Harrison, Steve Horn, and Summer Moon Scriver, ©2016. Front cover by Robert S. Harrison, ©2014. Back cover by Summer Moon Scriver (l), Steve Horn (c), Robert S. Harrison (r)©2014.

Acknowledgments

BOUNTY—Lopez Island Farmers, Food, and Community is a community-funded project. We are extremely grateful to these individual supporters and organizations who helped make this local food project possible. With special thanks to Sue Roundy for her vision and perseverance from start to finish.

Karen and Gary Alexander
Maria Armstrong
Greg Arquette
Jan Belson
David Bill and Faith Van de Putte
Peggy Bill
Susan Bill
Margaret and Jim Birkemeier
Karen Barringer and Linda Brower
Dena Brownstein and David Williams
Doug Benoliel and Tamara Buchanan
Glen Coye and Mary Wondra
Hilary Dahl
Diane Dear and Todd Goldsmith
Danielle and Garrett Devier
Nicole and Stephan Dietrich
Erin Eichler
Ande and Scott Finley
Iris and Jerry Graville
Rachel Graville
Chuenchom and Chris Greacen
Kitty Harmon and John Fulford
Polly Ham and Steve Horn
Esther Handy
Heather and Robert Harrison
Levanne Hendrix
Melora and Henryk Hiller
Linda and David Hudson
Kay and George Keeler
Marianne and Read Langenbach
Teri Linneman and Liz Scranton
Wendy McClure
Michelle McDarmont and Audrey Swanberg
Denise Doyle-McDougall and Stewart
   McDougall
Karyn McKelvey
Eliza Medearis and John Williams
Ron Metcalf

Scott Meyers and Brigit Waring
Clarissa and Charles Mish
Cynthia Moffitt
Kim and Ciro Pasciuto
Theodore Phillips
Page Read and Marney Reynolds
Jessica Roundy
Yuki and Kevin Seda-Kane
Diana and Ed Sheridan
Brady Simmons
Lexi and Kirman Taylor
Julie and Rip Van Camp
Nancy and Brian Voris
Nancy Wallace and Rich Youde

Special thanks to our Publishing Partners and generous BOUNTY friends:

Linda Barton
Inez Black
Toby Bright and Nancy Ward
Betsy and Peter Currie
Randall Dickson and Ron Walters
Birte and Jim Falconer
Anne Hietbrink and Beth Shirk
Lynn Hayes and Nancy Nordoff
Michele and Steve Heller
Suzi and Scott Jennings
Lopez Artists Guild
Lopez Community Land Trust
Lopez Locavores
Lopez Thrift Shop
Timothy Maxson and Don Smith
Pamela and Bob McCabe
Sue and Dale Roundy
Lauren and Jamie Stephens
Barbara and Dave Thomas
Raiti Waerness, to honor Heather and Robert's work

BOUNTY recipes were photographed at Kim and Ciro Pasciuto's outdoor kitchen, Rita O'Boyle's home, and Windy Bottom Farm. Thank you!

Profits from the sale of this book are donated to the Lopez School L.I.F.E. Garden Program where Lopez kids grow and eat nutritious, fresh food.